A COLLECTOR'S GUIDE TO

The Waffen-SS

Robin Lumsden

Acknowledgements
Thanks are due to the directors and staff of the following institutions for their generous help in supplying documentary and photographic material: Berlin Document Centre, Berlin; Hoffmann Bildarchiv, Munich; Imperial War Museum, London; Ullstein Bilderdienst, Berlin; US Army, Washington; West Point Museum, New York.

Special appreciation goes to Alan Lauder of Norval (Photographers) Ltd, Dunfermline, Fife, for his skilful assistance in photographing surviving examples of SS regalia from my own collection.

Last, but not least, a big *'danke'* to Grace, David and Iain for putting up with the rattle of the typewriter over the years.

Robin Lumsden
Cairneyhill
October 1993

Front Cover: *Camouflage field tunic and 'crusher' cap as worn by a Waffen-SS infantry Obersturmführer, 1944-45.*

Back Cover: *Wartime recruiting poster exhorting 17-year-old Germans to volunteer for service with the Waffen-SS.*

Other books by the same author and in the 'Collector's Guide' series.
A Collector's Guide to Third Reich Militaria
216mm x 146mm 192pp 0 7110 2669 6

A Collector's Guide to Third Reich Militaria: Detecting the Fakes
216mm x 146mm 192pp 0 7110 2670 X

Available from all good bookshops, or through mail order by writing to:
Ian Allan Publishing, Mail Order Dept,
Unit 3 Maizefield, Hinckley LE10 1YF.
Tel: 01455 233747.
Fax: 01455 233737.
E-mail: midlandbooks@compuserve.com

Please quote the reference number when ordering through mail order.

First published 1994
Reprinted 2000

ISBN 0 7110 2285 2

Published by Ian Allan Publishing

an imprint of Ian Allan Publishing Ltd,
Terminal House, Shepperton,
Surrey TW17 8AS

Printed by Ian Allan Printing Ltd, Riverdene Business Park, Hersham, Surrey KT12 4RG.

Contents

4. Waffen-SS Insignia 103

5. Reproductions, Fakes & Fantasies 143

Introduction

Of all the fighting formations which saw action in World War 2, those of the Third Reich have consistently attracted the most attention from the world's military enthusiasts, whether they be collectors, modellers, or those with just a general interest in the period. The reasons for this have never been too clear, but doubtless owe much to the splendour of the uniforms and regalia of Hitler's forces, combined with their spectacular achievements in battle. Germany did, after all, produce the highest ever scoring air, sea and land aces of any country during the 1939-45 period, exemplified by men like the Luftwaffe's Stuka pilot Hans-Ulrich Rudel, who flew 2,530 aerial combat sorties; fighter pilot Erich Hartmann, who shot down 352 Allied aircraft and was only 23 years old when the war ended; naval officer Wolfgang Lüth, whose submarine sent to the bottom 260,000 tons of enemy shipping; and the army soldier Günter Viezenz, who personally destroyed 21 tanks in single combat using only infantry weapons. Such men achieved tallies which will probably never be surpassed.

Even in such renowned company, the Waffen-SS continues to hold a position of unique interest. Many books on the subject have appeared over the years, from general histories to multi-volume day-by-day accounts of the wartime actions of individual units. The early views on Hitler's 'asphalt soldiers' concentrated on the theme of crime and criminality, describing how racial indoctrination made front-line SS units susceptible to many kinds of inhumane warfare. Much emphasis was placed on the atrocities at Malmédy, Oradour-sur-Glane and elsewhere. More recent analyses, on the other hand, have tended to reappraise the Waffen-SS as an élite multi-national fighting force, even a forerunner of NATO, composed of soldiers like any others who frequently emerged victorious against overwhelming odds and earned the respect both of their Wehrmacht comrades and of their enemies.

The purpose of this book is to offer guidance to collectors and others particularly interested in the subject of Waffen-SS uniforms and insignia. It is unfortunate that original Waffen-SS items are now becoming exceedingly scarce, a situation exacerbated by the fact that the collector's market has been flooded with fakes of varying qualities since the late 1950s. For that reason, some reliance has had to be placed on using wartime photographs to show genuine uniforms in wear. All examples of Waffen-SS regalia selected to illustrate this book are considered to be genuine, with the exception of the items shown in Chapter 5: Reproductions, Fakes and Fantasies.

Readers keen to learn more about the history and combat record of the Waffen-SS are referred to the bibliography. Moreover, for a detailed coverage of the organisation and influence of the SS as a whole, particularly the non-military Allgemeine-SS this book's companion volume, *The Black Corps*, (Ian Allan Ltd, 1992) is highly recommended.

1

1 Origins of the Waffen-SS, 1933-39

THE SCHUTZSTAFFEL DER NSDAP

After the defeat of Germany in November 1918, the government collapsed, revolution swept the country and politics became a dangerous business, with all sides employing strong-arm tactics. The stewards for the inaugural meeting of Adolf Hitler's Nazi Party or NSDAP (Nationalsozialistische Deutsche Arbeiterpartei) on 24 February 1920 were a squad of Zeitfreiwilligen or temporary volunteers, armed with pistols and clad in the field-grey of the Munich Reichswehr to which they were attached. Such guardsman might well have been sympathetic, but they certainly had no undying loyalty to the new movement. Thus, toward the end of 1920, a permanent and regular Nazi formation called the Saalschutz or Hall Guard was set up, to protect speakers at NSDAP meetings. In November 1921, the various Saalschutz groups throughout Bavaria were consolidated and renamed Sturmabteilungen or SA, after the élite German army assault detachments of World War I.

Everything in the early SA was *ad hoc* and improvised, and in return for securing the organising abilities of Ernst Röhm and other military sponsors Hitler had to let his 'Party troops' slip under the aegis of the Freikorps and Reichswehr. In March 1923, therefore, he ordered the formation of a headquarters guard or Stabswache, comprising 12 bodyguards loyal to him alone. Two months later, the Stabswache cadre was integrated into a new body known as the Stosstrupp, again named after the shock troops of World War 1. The Stosstrupp Hitler played its part in the abortive Munich Putsch on 9 November 1923, when one of its members was among the fallen.

On his release from prison in December 1924, Hitler began to rebuild his shattered Party. In February 1925 the NSDAP was reconstituted and the SA reactivated in an unarmed form. However, there was still no national SA, which remained at that stage little more than a social club for young roughnecks. In March, on the advice of Stosstrupp veteran Julius Schreck, Hitler recommended to local Party leaders the setting up of small guard details on the model of the Stabswache. They were to be known as Schutzstaffeln or protection squads, a new term subject to none of the governmental prohibitions and not identified with the old Freikorps traditions. The Schutzstaffel der NSDAP, soon abbreviated to SS, was to comprise 10-man squads selected from the most reliable local Party members. Applicants needed to be aged between 25 and 35 years, have two Nazi sponsors, and be of good character and powerful physique. Their sole purpose would be to protect Hitler and other Nazi leaders during their political campaigning throughout Germany. On 9 November 1925 the existence of the SS was officially pro-

Plate 1: *Sepp Dietrich in 1930, as head of the SS in Upper Bavaria. He wears an impressive array of decorations, including the Bavarian Military Merit Cross with Crown and Swords, the Iron Cross 1st and 2nd Classes, the Silesian Eagle and the Tank Battle Badge instituted on 13 July 1921. The latter was awarded to the 100 or so surviving combat veterans of the World War 1 German Panzer Corps, which in its entirety had comprised a total of only 20 A7V tanks. Dietrich served as an NCO on tank No 560, codenamed 'Alter Fritz', which was blown up the day before the war ended. He subsequently wore the Tank Battle Badge with pride throughout his service in the SS and was, in fact, the only recipient known to have been photographed wearing it.*

claimed in a ceremony at the Munich Feldherrnhalle.

In the spring of 1926, 75 Schutzstaffeln were formed right across the country. A new SS-Oberleitung was created, and the former Stosstrupp leader Josef Berchtold was nominated to head it with the self-styled title of Reichsführer der SS. However, he rapidly lost interest and in March 1927 relinquished his office to Erhard Heiden. Despite the extension of its numbers and theoretical prestige, the SS remained a limited organisation subordinated to the SA. Photographs dating from 1926 to 1929 rarely show as many as 10 SS men together. The SS were constantly intermingled with far more numerous SA members, although often in positions of prominence.

Amid charges in the Social Democratic Press that Heiden had been sacked for being a police spy, which Hitler denied, Heinrich Himmler was made Reichsführer der SS on 6 January 1929 and tasked with consolidating the scattered SS membership. The SS was duly accorded its own higher officer corps (until then there had simply been SS-Führer and no non-commissioned officers) on the lines of the SA. Among the new SS leadership was Josef 'Sepp' Dietrich, who became the Scharführer, or Gau SS Leader, of Upper Bavaria.

The SS grew steadily during 1930-32 within the matrix of a rapidly expanding SA and NSDAP membership. The 1931 revolt of SA-Oberführer Walther Stennes and his cohorts underscored the value of SS units independent of SA dominance. Over a period of time the SS gradually became better prepared than the SA for street confrontations, better disciplined *vis à vis* the police, and better controlled. Early in 1931, Himmler kept busy changing and rechanging his unit designations to keep up with the elaborate tables of organisation being constructed by Röhm and his staff. The SS Stürme had scarcely been given arabic numerals when those had to be reassigned to Standarten. Weak SS companies became even weaker SS regiments, and 30 small SS regiments became tiny SS brigades. The brigade system was then abandoned altogether and light, purely administrative, units known as Oberführer-Abschnitte were interposed between about 40 Standarten and the Reichsführer-SS.

By April 1932, the SS had expanded to incorporate 450 officers and 25,000 men. During that year the political struggle in Germany rapidly took on the form of a civil war. The Communist Party and Socialists set up armed militias and the SA and SS responded. Ten SS men were killed and several hundreds wounded during street battles with the Red Front. The whole scenario was lapped up by the SS Old Guard, and their catch-phrase 'Die Kampfzeit war die beste Zeit' ('The fighting days were the best') was frequently repeated as a form of boast to young SS men well into the Third Reich period.

As the crucial 1933 elections approached, it suited the Nazis to create the impression that Germany was on the verge of anarchy and that they had all the solutions. Not surprisingly, they won a great electoral victory and on 30 January the old Field Marshal Paul von Hindenburg, President of the Reich, entrusted Hitler with the post of Chancellor and the responsibility of forming a government. On 28 February, less than a month after the assumption of power, the Reichstag was burned to the ground and the Communists were blamed. The next day Hitler issued a 'Decree for the Protection of People and State' giving police powers to the SA and SS. Firearms were issued to 25,000 SA and 15,000 SS men acting as Hilfspolizei or Auxiliary Policemen, and left-wing opponents began to be herded into makeshift prisons and camps. From that time on, the SS split into two distinct groups: the traditional Allgemeine-SS which was basically part-time and fulfilled a police function; and the new Bewaffnete-SS or Armed SS which was full-time and military in character. It is on the latter group that the remainder of this book will concentrate.

Plate 2: *Men of the Sonderkommando Zossen enjoying a break from their rigorous training at Essenfassen, summer 1933. All wear black 'krätzchen' field caps and the grey cotton drill fatigue uniform.* Imperial War Museum (IWM)

When Hitler assumed the Chancellorship, he felt that he could not entirely rely on the traditional Reichswehr and police guards appointed by the State to protect him. Consequently, he quickly issued instructions for the formation of a new full-time armed SS unit whose sole function would be to escort him at all times, whether in Berlin or on his official journeys throughout Germany. The task of forming the unit was entrusted to Sepp Dietrich, who by that time had risen to the rank of SS-Gruppenführer through his position as one of Hitler's closest personal friends.

By 17 March 1933, Dietrich had hand-picked 120 loyal SS volunteers, including a few former members of the Stosstrupp Hitler, to become the nucleus of a new headquarters guard called the SS Stabswache 'Berlin'. They were armed with rifles and initially quartered in the Alexander Barracks on Friedrichstrasse, not far from Hitler's official residence, the Reich Chancellery. In May, the Stabswache was enlarged and reformed as the SS Sonderkommando Zossen, with three training companies. In addition to guard duties, this 'Special Force' could now also be used for armed police and anti-terrorist tasks. The following month, three new companies were recruited as the SS Sonderkommando Jüterbog and at the Party Day Rally in September 1933 both detachments were merged into a single formation and renamed the Leibstandarte-SS 'Adolf Hitler' or LAH, which may best be translated as the 'Adolf Hitler' Life Guards, invoking memories of the famed Bavarian Royal Bodyguard Regiments. On 9 November 1933, in front of the Feldherrnhalle, the Leibstandarte took a personal oath of loyalty to its Führer. There could now be no doubt that these men, unlike the soldiers of the Reichswehr, were Hitler's personal troops.

As an SS unit, the Leibstandarte theoretically came under the overall control of Heinrich Himmler. However, in practice, Hitler considered himself to be the ultimate director of its actions. That fact, combined with Dietrich's friendship with Hitler, which the guard commander exploited to the full, ensured that the Leibstandarte enjoyed a fair measure of independence within the SS organisation. Indeed, the prewar Leibstandarte ultimately became, in Himmler's own words, 'a complete law unto itself'. Dietrich frequently argued with the Reichsführer, whom he addressed as an equal, a luxury enjoyed by very few SS officers.

In late 1933, the LAH moved into quarters at Berlin-Lichterfelde from where squads of troops were sent to the Reich Chancellery on a rota basis to provide a smart, impressive and effective bodyguard for the Führer. An order at the end of the year introduced their then very distinctive insignia of un-numbered SS runes on the right collar patch and a cuff title bearing the name 'Adolf Hitler'. The Leibstandarte came to be in exclusive prominence around

3

Plate 3: *SS-Gruppenführer Sepp Dietrich, commander of Hitler's bodyguard, at the end of 1933. Dietrich has removed the SS armband from his black service uniform, which was a short-term expedient adopted during this period to set personnel of the infant Leibstandarte apart from the mass of the Allgemeine-SS.*

4

Hitler, its men serving not only as his guards but also as his adjutants, drivers, servants and waiters. Their ceremonial activities ultimately became almost legendary, and their performance on the drill square and at Nazi rallies, where they consistently held the place of honour at the end of the parade, was second to none.

On 30 June 1934, the Leibstandarte helped quell the so-called Röhm Putsch and was largely responsible for the killing of many of Hitler's enemies within the SA in the 'Night of the Long Knives'. Many of those arrested were taken to the Lichterfelde Barracks which became a clearing house for unwanted people and corpses. It is not known precisely how many 'enemies of the State' were shot by Leibstandarte firing squads, but it is thought that there were some 40 executioners involved. The shooting finally ended on 2 July and the Leibstandarte's first action was over. That day, Hitler promised Dietrich that the LAH would be expanded into a fully-equipped regiment as a reward for its services.

Early in October 1934 it was decided that the Leibstandarte should be motorised, a rare honour in days when the majority of the Reichswehr was still horse-drawn. By the end of the month, the LAH consisted of:

- 1 Staff
- 3 Motorised Infantry Battalions
- 1 Motorcycle Company
- 1 Mortar Company
- 1 Signals Platoon
- 1 Armoured Car Platoon
- 1 Regimental Band

Plate 4: *Leibstandarte sentry at the courtyard entrance to the new Reich Chancellery, November 1938. The LAH, being a guards regiment, spent much of its time on ceremonial duties for which distinctive white leather equipment, comprising waist belt, cross-strap, ammunition pouches, bayonet frog, pistol holster and pack straps, was introduced in stages from 1936.*

Plate 5: *A Leibstandarte battalion parades past Hitler on his 50th birthday, 20 April 1939. Note the white leather gauntlets worn by the officers in the colour party.*

It was a relatively short step from being equipped and trained for anti-terrorist police duties to being organised for military activities and the Leibstandarte was soon wearing field-grey. Given its largely ceremonial background, it is surprising just how quickly the LAH developed into a first class military unit and how far it assimilated itself within the rest of the Armed SS. On 7 March 1936 it played a leading role in the first of Hitler's expansionist moves when it provided the advance guard in the occupation of the demilitarised zone of the Rhineland. Two years later, a motorised battalion of the LAH took part in the annexation of Austria, the so-called Anschluss. It moved through Linz, where it provided a Guard of Honour for Hitler, and on to Vienna, taking part in the triumphal celebrations there. The Austrian operation meant that the Leibstandarte had covered no less than 600 miles in some 48 hours in full co-operation with the army, a high military ability which earned the favourable recognition of no less a commander than General Guderian. Seven months later the LAH participated in the occupation of the Sudetenland and again the whole event proceeded smoothly.

At the time of the German invasion of Poland in September 1939, the Leibstandarte comprised:

- 1 Staff (with signals platoon, motorcycle dispatch platoon and band)
- 3 Motorised Infantry Battalions
- 1 Motorised Infantry Gun Company
- 1 Motorised Anti-tank Company
- 1 Motorcycle Company
- 1 Motorised Engineer Platoon
- 1 Armoured Car Platoon

In addition to these field units, there was also a fourth Guard Battalion (IV Wach-Bataillon) maintained in Berlin-Lichterfelde to guard the Chancellery and Hitler's mountain retreat at Obersalzberg. All elements of the LAH, except for the Guard Battalion and a replacement unit, were to take part in the opening stages of World War 2.

As the first Armed SS unit, the Leibstandarte was destined to hold a proud place as the oldest and smartest formation in the Waffen-SS, and was to earn itself a formidable fighting record at the front.

At the same time as the infant Leibstandarte was being formed to protect Hitler, other small groups of armed SS men were set up all over Germany as a means of bolstering the new régime in the event of civil unrest or counter-revolution. As a general rule, each SS Abschnitt recruited its own Kasernierte Hundertschaft of 100 or so barracked troops, and several of these were amalgamated in key areas to become company or even battalion-sized Politische Bereitschaften or PBs, Political Reserve Squads. The entire country was eventually covered by a network of PBs, some of which played a significant part in the 'Night of the Long Knives'. On 24 September 1934 Hitler announced that the Politische Bereitschaften were to be brought together and expanded into a new force to be called the SS-Verfügungstruppe or SS-VT, political troops at the special disposal of the Nazi régime. The SS-VT would be formed on the basis of three Standarten modelled on army infantry regiments, each to comprise three battalions, a motorcycle company and a mortar company. In addition, an SS-VT signals battalion would act in a supporting role. The new formation was to be under the command of the Reichsführer-SS for internal security duties, except in time of war when it would be at the disposal of the army.

The picture of a new Imperial Guard attracted many ex-officers into the ranks of the Verfügungstruppe. SA-Standartenführer Paul Hausser, a former Reichswehr General, was recruited by Himmler to organise the SS-VT and instil some military know-how into the SS soldiers. In October 1934 a cadet school was opened at Bad Tölz, and early the following year Hausser took personal charge of the second officer training establishment at Braunschweig. Hausser's solid groundwork attracted a sufficient number of ex-army and police officers, redundant Reichswehr sergeant-majors and young military enthusiasts to form the officer and NCO cadres of the future Waffen-SS. The cadres were distributed to the scattered SS-VT battalions and these were gradually formed into regiments. In Munich, three Sturmbanne amalgamated to become SS-Standarte I/VT,

Fig 1: *Styles of SS-VT uniform in 1937. These are, from left to right:*
(i) Field service uniform for SS-Sturmmann
(ii) Sports kit

Plate 6: *NCOs of the SS-VT signals battalion in October 1935. All wear the 'SS/lightning bolt' collar patch, which looks like three Sig-runes from a distance, and the blank cuff title sported by personnel of this unit until the introduction of the 'SS-Nachrichtensturmbann' title in 1937.*

6

FIG 1

Dienstanzug der SS-Verfüg.-Truppe
SS-Sturmmann

SS-Sportanzug

FIG 1A

Paradeanzug der SS-Verfüg.-Truppe
SS-Scharführer

Dienstanzug, Mantel
SS-Oberführer

Plate 7: *Hilmar Wäckerle, commander of Sturmbann I, SS-VT Standarte 'Germania', as depicted by Wolfgang Willrich in 1936. Note the 'SS/small 2' collar patch. Wäckerle had formerly been the first commandant of Dachau concentration camp, and in 1938 transferred to the 'Der Führer' regiment to lead its 3rd battalion. He was later killed in action while commanding 'Westland' on the Eastern Front.*

organised and equipped as a horse-drawn infantry regiment. It was given the honour title 'Deutschland' at the Nürnberg Rally in September 1935. Members subsequently wore the SS runes alongside a '1' on the right collar patch, and a 'Deutschland' cuff title. In Hamburg, another three Sturmbanne duly came together to constitute SS-Standarte 2/VT, which was named 'Germania' at Nürnberg in September 1936. The regimental uniform was characterised by an 'SS 2' collar patch and 'Germania' cuff title.

On 1 October 1936, Hausser was appointed Inspector of Verfügungstruppe with the rank of SS-Brigadeführer. He created a divisional staff to supervise the equipping and training of his troops and avidly welcomed newcomers who brought the promise of a certain dynamism to the SS-VT. Foremost among these was SS-Sturmbannführer Felix Steiner, an ex-Reichswehr officer whose experiences on the Western Front in World War 1 had turned him against the conservative doctrines of Hausser and the army. He favoured the tactics of assault detachments, shock troops and mobile battle groups, to escape from the deadly immobility of trench warfare with one mass army facing another in a mutual battle of attrition. Steiner was given command of the SS-VT Standarte 'Deutschland' and tried out his reforms with one of its battalions, the training of which centred on sports and athlet-

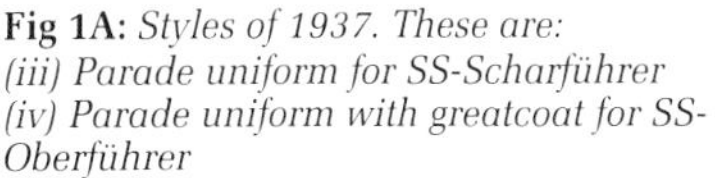

Fig 1A: *Styles of 1937. These are:*
(iii) Parade uniform for SS-Scharführer
(iv) Parade uniform with greatcoat for SS-Oberführer

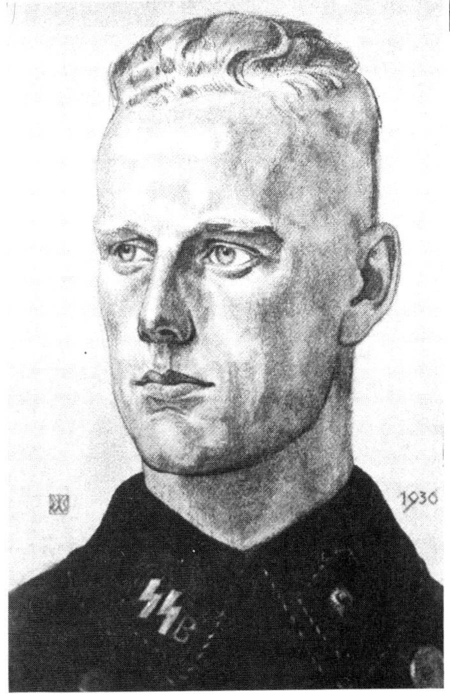

Plate 8: *Willrich print showing the 'SS/B' collar patch being worn by an Unterscharführer on the staff of the SS Officers' School at Braunschweig in 1936.*

9

Plate 9: *An SS-VT soldier wearing the earth-grey uniform in 1936. Note the black/aluminium twisted cord piping on the greatcoat collar, and the newly-introduced 1935-model steel helmet.*

ics. Officers, NCOs and men competed in teams against each other, to promote a spirit of comradeship and eliminate differences in rank. Experiments were carried out with camouflage clothing and Steiner replaced the army's regulation rifle with handier and more mobile weapons, primarily sub-machine guns and hand grenades. Soon even the Wehrmacht's eyebrows rose as Steiner's troops covered almost two miles in 20 minutes in battle order, for such a thing was unheard of. Steiner implanted in his men the idea that they were a military élite and the success of his modernisation was so obvious that the Verfügungstruppe began to look upon him as their real commander. According to a somewhat jealous Hausser, Himmler considered Steiner to be 'his favourite baby'.

After the annexation of Austria in March 1938, in which 'Germania' participated, Hitler ordered that a new SS-VT Standarte be formed entirely from Austrian personnel, either newly recruited or transferred from other SS-VT units. The resultant regiment was given the honour title 'Der Führer' at the Nürnberg Rally in September1938, and members were distinguished by an appropriately named cuff title and 'SS3' collar patch.

During the mobilisation preceding the occupation of the Sudetenland in October 1938, 'Deutschland' and 'Germania' were placed under the command of the army and took part in the operation. All the SS-VT Standarten became motorised regiments at the end of the year and in the spring of 1939 were used to fill the gaps in a number of armoured divisions which invaded Czechoslovakia. In May, 'Deutschland' went on exercise at the Münsterlager training area where it carried out extremely tough and hazardous manoeuvres using live ammunition. Hitler, who was present, was so impressed that he gave his permission for the expansion of the SS-Verfügungstruppe into a full division. The idea was temporarily postponed, however, as units of the SS-VT were integrated with those of the army in preparation for the attack on Poland.

By the outbreak of World War 2, the SS-VT comprised not only the 'Deutschland', 'Germania' and 'Der Führer' Standarten, but also an artillery regiment, SS-Regiment z.b.V. 'Ellwangen' for special employment, a signals battalion, a pioneer battalion, the so-called SS-Sturmbann 'N' which was garrisoned at Nürnberg and provided a guard at the annual Nazi Party rallies, a reconnaissance battalion, an anti-aircraft machine gun battalion and an anti-tank battalion. There were also a number of replacement units, or Ersatzeinheiten, whose purpose was to make good any wartime losses suffered by the SS-VT.

The SS-Verfügungstruppe provided valuable military experience for many SS officers who were later to become prominent personalities in the divisions of the Waffen-SS.

Plate 10: *A battalion of SS-VT Standarte 'Deutschland' parading before Hitler in 1937. Swallow's nests distinguish the regimental bandsmen in the foreground.*

Plate 11: *The two Feldzeichen and six battalion flags of the Leibstandarte-SS 'Adolf Hitler' and SS-VT Standarte 'Deutschland' on display at Nürnberg, September 1937. All the standard-bearers wear gorgets and bandoliers.*

10

11

12

Plate 12: *NCOs and men of Sturmbann III, SS-VT Standarte 'Germania', outside their barracks at Radolfzell in 1938.*

In March 1933 Himmler set up the first independent SS-run concentration camp at Dachau to accommodate 5,000 of the 27,000 potential 'enemies of the State' arrested by the SA and SS after the Reichstag Fire. Men of the local Allgemeine-SS were seconded to a new SS-Wachverbände or Guard Unit under SS-Oberführer Theodor Eicke to supervise the inmates of Dachau, who were to be incarcerated on a long-term basis. By the summer of 1934, most of the semi-official SA detention camps throughout Germany had been closed and as a direct result of the 'Night of the Long Knives', during which Eicke personally killed Ernst Röhm, the remaining camps were removed from the jurisdiction of the SA and civil authorities and were permanently taken over by the SS.

At first, the SS-Wachverbände staffing the concentration camps were lightly armed and used by the Allgemeine-SS as depositories for unwanted personnel. Eicke, however, turned Dachau into a model camp and in July 1934 he was promoted to SS-Gruppenführer and made Inspekteur der Konzentrationslager (Inspector of all Concentration Camps) with the task of improving the discipline and morale of the SS-Wachverbände. This he accomplished with some considerable success. By March 1935, with an increasing number of new camps opening up to accommodate more and more prisoners, the Wachverbände had expanded to incorporate the following company-sized units, each assigned to a particular camp:

- SS-Wachtruppe 'Oberbayern' (Dachau)
- SS-Wachtruppe 'Ostfriesland' (Esterwegen)
- SS-Wachtruppe 'Elbe' (Lichtenburg)
- SS-Wachtruppe 'Sachsen' (Sachsenburg)
- SS-Wachtruppe 'Brandenburg' (Oranienburg and Columbia-Haus)
- SS-Wachtruppe 'Hansa' (Hamburg-Fuhlsbüttel)

During 1935, these formations were completely removed from the control of the Allgemeine-SS and reorganised into five independent battalions, namely:

- SS-Wachsturmbann I 'Oberbayern' (Dachau)
- SS-Wachsturmbann II 'Elbe' (Lichtenburg)
- SS-Wachsturmbann III 'Sachsen' (Sachsenburg)
- SS-Wachsturmbann IV 'Ostfriesland' (Esterwegen)
- SS-Wachsturmbann V 'Brandenburg' (Oranienburg and Columbia-Haus)

On 29 March 1936, the Wachsturmbanne, with a strength of 3,500 men, were collectively renamed the SS-Totenkopfverbände or SS-TV (SS Death's Head Units) and allocated distinctive new collar patches. On 1 July 1937 they were regrouped into the following three regiments, comprising 4,500 men:

- SS-Totenkopfstandarte 1 "Oberbayern' at Dachau
- SS-Totenkopfstandarte 2 'Brandenburg' at Sachsenhausen
- SS-Totenkopfstandarte 3 'Thüringen' at Buchenwald

In 1938 a fourth regiment SS-Totenkopfstandarte 4 'Ostmark', was formed in Austria to staff the new camp at Mauthausen.

Eicke, as a former paymaster of the Imperial Army, had an undying hatred of the professional officers whom he saw in command of the SS-Verfügungstruppe and one of his objects was to turn the Totenkopfverbände into a sort of brutal working-class counterforce to the SS-VT. Himmler had given him almost complete autonomy in his appointment as Inspekteur der Konzentrationslager and Eicke kept a jealous watch to ensure than no senior ex-officers infiltrated his organisation to threaten his position. While his troops were heavily armed on army lines, albeit with rather outdated weaponry, Eicke continually warned them against any attempt to ape a military organisation, and he frequently impressed upon them that they belonged neither to the army nor the police nor to the Verfügungstruppe. Their sole task was to isolate the 'enemies of the State' from the German people. Eicke drummed

Plate 13: *SS-Gruppenführer Albert Forster, Gauleiter of Danzig-West Prussia, reviewing the SS-Heimwehr Danzig in August 1939. The officer on the left is SS-Obersturmbannführer Friedmann Götze, commander of the Heimwehr, who was killed by a British sniper at Le Paradis on 28 May 1940, while serving with the SS-Totenkopf-Division.*

the concept of dangerous subversives so forcefully and convincingly into his men that they became firmly convinced of their position as the Reich's true guardians. They were the only soldiers who even in peacetime faced the enemy day and night . . . the enemy behind the wire.

The regulations governing the Totenkopfverbände became ever stricter. Any member allowing a prisoner to escape would be handed over to the Gestapo. Prisoners who tried to escape would be shot without warning, as would any inmate who assaulted a guard. The main forms of punishment in the camps were beatings, hard labour and tying prisoners to trees, and there were several instances of inmates being killed by SS-TV guards, whose hatred of the prisoners was consciously cultivated. Most Totenkopf men were under 20 years of age and almost 95 per cent of them were unmarried, with little or no personal ties.

By 1939, the SS-Totenkopfverbände had grown to include SS-Totenkopfstandarte 5 'Dietrich Eckart', a medical battalion, an anti-tank demonstration company, a motorised signals platoon, and a semi-motorised engineer unit. Whatever Eicke may have intended, his SS-TV had developed into a truly military organisation and on 17 August Hitler recognised the fact by ordering that in the event of war the Totenkopfstandarten should be used as police reinforcements within the framework of the Wehrmacht (ie as occupation troops) and that their task of guarding the concentration camps should be taken over by older Allgemeine-SS reservists formed into new SS-Totenkopf-Wachsturmbanne. The third battalion of SS-Totenkopfstandarte 4 had already taken up a defensive position as a Home Guard unit in Danzig, the so-called SS-Heimwehr Danzig, and was bolstered by a reserve battalion, SS-Wachsturmbann Eimann. At the same time, 10,000 younger officers and men of the Allgemeine-SS were called up for service with the Death's Head Units.

When World War 2 broke out the following month, the plan to use Eicke's men as occupation troops was quickly modified. Dachau was cleared of inmates and the Totenkopfstandarten, augmented by the young Allgemeine-SS conscripts and some police personnel, were mustered there and formed into the SS-Totenkopf-Division for combat service alongside the Leibstandarte and SS-VT. Death's Head troops were soon to gain a reputation as some of the hardest and most ruthless front-line soldiers of the war.

Volunteers to join the prewar SS-VT and SS-TV had to be between the ages of 17 and 22, at least 5ft 11in tall and of the highest physical fitness. Entry requirements for the Leibstandarte were even more stringent, with a minimum height of 6ft 1in, and it was no idle boast of Himmler's that until 1936 even a filled tooth was adjudged a sufficient deformity to disqualify a young man from entry into the Führer's Guard. Needless to say, as with ordinary members of the Allgemeine-SS, Aryan pedigree had to be spotless.

From 1935, membership of the Leibstandarte and SS-Verfügungstruppe counted as military service, and rates of pay corresponded to those of the Wehrmacht. However, terms were hard. Enlisted men had to sign up for a minimum of four years, NCOs for 12 years and officers for 25 years. Moreover, they were all subject to the SS legal system and discipline code, and were obliged to secure the Reichsführer's permission before they could marry. Membership of the Totenkopfverbände, while similarly demanding in terms of service conditions, did not count as fulfilment of military duty until the spring of 1939. Before that time, SS-VT volunteers had to complete their statutory term of military conscription either in the Wehrmacht or SS-Verfügungstruppe. Eicke preferred his men to do their service in the army, navy or air force as he was concerned that if they were to join the SS-VT they might not want to return to the onerous task of guarding concentration camps.

Once in the Armed SS, recruits were moulded into very adaptable soldier-athletes capable of much better than average endurance on the march and in combat. Great emphasis was placed upon ideological indoctrination, physical exercise and sports, which were made integral and continual parts of the training programme and daily life. More time was spent in the field, on the ranges and in the classroom learning the theory of tactics than was the practice in the army, while considerably less attention was given to drill, even in the Leibstandarte after 1938. This resulted in a standard of battlefield movement and shooting that was appreciably higher than that of the Wehrmacht. Manoeuvres were made as realistic as possible, with the use of live ammunition and heavy artillery barrages, so that every SS-VT man became fully accustomed to handling a variety of weapons and also to being within 100 yards of explosions from his own artillery fire. The end product was a higher standard of soldier, a man who was a storm-trooper in the best traditions of the term.

Unlike their counterparts in the army, SS rank-and-file were taught to think for themselves and not rely too heavily on the issuance of orders from above. Consequently, they became very self-reliant. Every SS man was looked upon as a potential NCO, and every NCO as a potential officer. Officer cadets, irrespective of background or social standing, had to serve two years in the ranks before proceeding to one of the military academies, or Junkerschulen, at Bad Tölz and Braunschweig. A

14

Plate 14: *Waffen-SS pay book and identity document, bearing the ubiquitous Sig-runes insignia.*

very tough training programme was undertaken at these institutions and by 1938-39 around 500 officers were being produced annually. The average SS-VT officer was considerably more aggressive in combat than his Wehrmacht colleagues, which is highlighted by the fact that nearly all of the first 54 cadets who passed out of Bad Tölz in 1934 were killed in battle between 1939 and 1942.

A final significant factor which contributed to the unique nature of the Armed SS was the atmosphere of camaraderie and 'heroic realism' which permeated its ranks. Soldiers of the SS were taught to be fighters for fighting's sake, and to abandon themselves to the struggle if so required for the greater good. The traditional soldierly concept was turned into one of pure belligerence, with the cultivation of a fatalistic enthusiasm for combat which far exceeded the normal self-sacrifice which might be expected of a soldier. That ethos went a long way to explain the particularly heavy casualties later suffered by the Waffen-SS during the war, and the determination and hardness of its survivors.

Soldiers of the Leibstandarte, SS-VT and SS-TV were eligible for the whole range of military orders, medals and awards created by the Nazi régime. Moreover, every SS recruit was expected to win the SA Military Sports Badge and the German National Sports Badge during his basic training. In addition to these national honours, a series of decorations was created specifically for the militarised formation of the SS, although full-time officials of the Allgemeine-SS were also eligible. These were the SS Dienstauszeichnungen or long service awards, instituted on 30 January 1938 and modelled on their Wehrmacht equivalents. The series comprised medals for four and eight years' service and large swastika-shaped 'crosses' for 12 and 25 years.

Photographic evidence indicates that the SS Dienstauszeichnungen were not widely distributed and, in fact, it is likely that presentations ceased around 1941 for the duration of the war. Himmler appears to have been virtually the only senior SS leader to consistently wear his decoration with pride. With the sole exception of Otto Kumm, the runic ribbon of the 12-year award was never seen on the tunic of any Waffen-SS General – Dietrich, Hausser and Steiner included – although they must have been entitled to wear it, particularly as service before 1933 and after 1939 counted as double for the purposes of presentation.

An SS Marksmanship Badge, for proficiency in rifle and machine-gun shooting, was approved prior to the outbreak of World War 2. The oval pin-on award, for wear on the right breast pocket, was to be presented in three grades, viz:

- 2nd Class (one oakleaf)
- 1st Class (two oakleaves)
- Sharpshooter (three oakleaves)

However, there is no evidence that the decoration was ever put into production. Examples which exist in private collections, bearing the maker marks of the Gahr firm, are thought to be fakes.

The so-called 'Gold Badge of the SS Technical Sergeant's Course', comprising a sword and oakleaves surmounted by an eagle, swastika, spanner and vehicle front, is also considered to be a postwar creation, based on the design featured at the top of a well-publicised Schirrmeister's certificate dating from 1943.

15

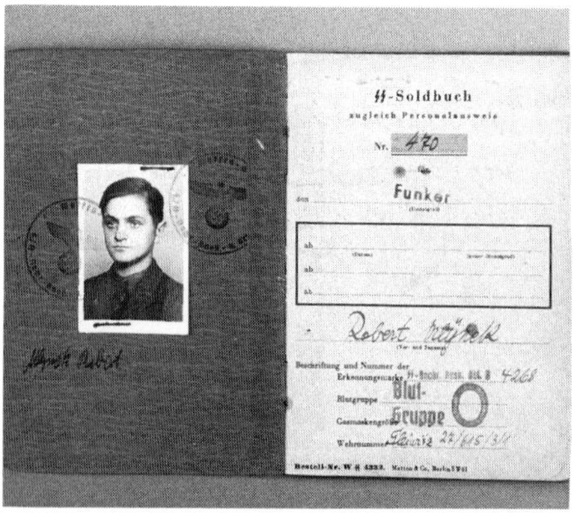

Plate 15: *Soldbuch issued in December 1944 to Robert Mlynek, a radio operator in the 4th Company of the 3rd SS Signals Training and Replacement Battalion, attached to 3rd SS-Panzer Division 'Totenkopf'.*

2 The Waffen-SS at War, 1939-45

THE BAPTISM OF FIRE, 1939-40

The SS was primarily a civil police force which Hitler hoped would eventually maintain order not only in Germany but also throughout Nazi-occupied Europe. The Führer decided that to do so, however, it would first have to win its spurs on the battlefield. As early as 1934, he told Himmler:

'In our Reich of the future, the SS and police will possess the necessary authority in their relations with other citizens only if they have a soldierly character. Through their past experience of glorious military events and their present education by the NSDAP, the German people have acquired such a warrior mentality that a fat, jovial sock-knitting police such as we had during the Weimar era can no longer exert authority. For this reason it will be necessary for our SS and police, in their own closed units, to prove themselves at the front in the same way as the army and to make blood sacrifices to the same degree as any other branch of the armed forces.'

All members of the Allgemeine-SS were subject to the normal term of military conscription into the Wehrmacht, which swallowed up the majority of SS men after the outbreak of war. Indeed, as early as January 1940 the Reichsführer announced that of approximately 250,000 regulars in the Allgemeine-SS at the opening of hostilities, almost 175,000 had since joined the Wehrmacht, with most going to the army. However, it was the actions of the Leibstandarte-SS 'Adolf Hitler', the SS-Verfügungstruppe and the SS-Totenkopfverbände which epitomised the early battlefield accomplishments of the SS in the eyes of the German public.

When German troops marched into Poland on 1 September 1939, the Armed SS units were split up among regular army formations dispersed along the invasion front. The SS-Heimwehr Danzig immediately secured that city, while other Totenkopf personnel cut through the 'Polish Corridor'. The Leibstandarte, supported by the SS-VT pioneer battalion, was attached to General von Reichenau's 10th Army. The SS-VT Standarte 'Deutschland', together with the SS artillery regiment and SS reconnaissance battalion, joined Generalmajor Kempf's 4th Panzer Brigade while 'Germania' became part of the 14th Army under General List. The 'Der Führer' Standarte was not yet fully trained and consequently did not participate in the fighting. Although 'Germania' remained in reserve for most of the four-week campaign, 'Deutschland' was heavily engaged in the Battle of Brest-Litovsk. The Leibstandarte also had a particularly hectic time, taking part in the drive on Warsaw and the encirclement of Bzura with 4th Panzer Division.

Despite the obvious fighting commitment of the SS, their disproportionately heavy casualties were criticised by the army who claimed the losses resulted from poor leadership. Hausser countered these accusations by indicating that, in order to operate efficiently, the Armed SS would need to be organised into full divisions. The army bitterly opposed such a development, but Hitler was persuaded to allow it in time for the western campaign.

At the end of 1939, the term 'Waffen-SS' began to be used on official correspondence when referring to the Armed SS, and in February 1940 it became official. About the same time, army desig-

nations such as 'Bataillon' and 'Regiment' generally replaced 'Sturmbann', 'Standarte' and the other SS formation titles. In some units of the SS-VT, army rank terms, for example Oberleutnant instead of SS-Obersturmführer, were even utilised for a short period, but that was quickly forbidden by Himmler. The purpose of all this was to assimilate the new force and make it easier for the army to accept the Waffen-SS as a legitimate fourth branch of the Wehrmacht, and one completely separate from the Allgemeine-SS.

Fig 2: *The unique Feldzeichen presented to the Leibstandarte-SS 'Adolf Hitler' in September 1940, in recognition of its success in the western blitzkrieg. The banner is based on Hitler's personal standard.*

The consolidation of the Waffen-SS during the so called 'Phoney War' brought Sepp Dietrich's Leibstandarte up to the strength of a superbly-equipped armoured regiment, and the three SS-VT regiments were formed into the first full SS division, the SS-Verfügungsdivision or SS-V, under the command of Paul Hausser. The SS-Totenkopfstandarten, supplemented by Allgemeine-SS and police conscripts, amalgamated to become the SS-Totenkopf-Division or SS-T, under Eicke, and a third combat division, the Polizei-Division led by SS-Brigadeführer Karl Pfeffer-Wildenbruch, was created almost overnight by a mass transfer of uniformed police personnel strengthened by cadres of SS-V and SS-T troops. The Polizei-Division was, however, intended to be very much a second-line security unit, and it was organised on the basis of horse-drawn infantry equipped with outdated Czech weapons.

The campaign in the west established beyond doubt the fighting reputation of the Waffen-SS. When the Blitzkrieg began in May 1940, the Leibstandarte and 'Der Führer' were deployed on the Dutch frontier and had little difficulty in sweeping through Holland, securing many vital river crossings as they went. On 16 May, SS-T went into action in support of Rommel's 7th Panzer Division in southern Belgium and eastern France, duly committing one of

Plate 16: *At the end of the 18-day Polish campaign, Hitler visited German troops at the battlefront, accompanied by his hand-picked SS bodyguard detachment, the so-called Führerbegleitkommando. Here one of the high-speed escort vehicles is passing a Wehrmacht convoy, forcing a local farmer into the side of the road. The machine-gunner, a LAH Untersturmführer, wears an NCO's 'crusher' field cap and dust goggles.*

Plate 17: *Assault engineers and artillery of the SS-Totenkopf-Division crossing La Bassée canal, 23 May 1940. Camouflage clothing had not been widely distributed to SS-T troops at this early stage in the war, and field-grey army pattern tunics with matching death's head collar patches were the order of the day.*

16

17

the first recorded SS atrocities when 100 unarmed British prisoners of the 2nd Royal Norfolks were machine-gunned at Le Paradis by inexperienced and panicky Totenkopf troops who had been thrown into disarray by the ferocity of a recent British counter-attack. The German advance soon divided the Allied forces into two, with large numbers of British, French and Belgian soldiers separated from the main bulk of the French army to the south of the 'panzer corridor'. The Leibstandarte, SS-V and SS-T were in the forefront of the sweep, and 'Deutschland' distinguished itself particularly well in some fiercely contested canal crossings. The northern Allies quickly became compressed into an ever-decreasing defensive pocket centring around Dunkirk. The Leibstandarte was heavily engaged in desperate fighting at the nearby village of Wormhoudt, where Sepp Dietrich was trapped in a burning ditch for several hours as the battle raged around him. A company of his men under Wilhelm Mohnke retaliated by killing 50 British prisoners-of-war in cold blood. After the Dunkirk evacuation, the Waffen-SS was redeployed against the main body of the French army which was holding a line along the River Somme. While the slow-moving Polizei-Division successfully slogged it out through the Argonne forest, other motorised SS units had little difficulty in smashing through enemy lines on 6 June and within a week the Leibstandarte had linked up with army panzers as far south as Vichy. The SS-Totenkopf-Division advanced on Bordeaux and the SS-Verfügungsdivision raced towards Biarritz. On 17 June the French sued for peace and five days later the war in the west was over.

In recognition of their bravery and leadership during the western campaign in 1940, the following seven SS men received the coveted Knight's Cross of the Iron Cross, at that time the supreme German military award:

- 25 June — SS-Brigadeführer Heinz Reinefarth, then serving as an army Feldwebel with Infantry Regiment 337
- 4 July — SS-Obergruppenführer Sepp Dietrich, commander Leibstandarte-SS 'Adolf Hitler'
- 15 August — SS-Oberführer Felix Steiner, commander SS-Regiment 'Deutschland'
- 15 August — SS-Oberführer Georg Keppler, commander SS-Regiment 'Der Führer'
- 4 September — SS-Hauptscharführer Ludwig Kepplinger, 11th Company, SS-Regiment 'Der Führer'

18

Plate 18: *A Leibstandarte machine-gun team marching through the French countryside, June 1940. Note the ubiquitous helmet covers and the MG34 toolcase attached to the belt of the man in the foreground.*

19

20

Plate 19: *SS-Totenkopf troops celebrate after the fall of France. The man on the right wears the white 'Hilfs-Krankenträger' armband of an auxiliary stretcher-bearer, and a typical mixture of clothing and insignia is evident from the appearance of the others. One soldier even wears contradictory rank badges, ie the blank left-hand collar patch of an SS-Schütze in conjunction with the arm chevron of an SS-Sturmmann!* IWM

Plate 20: *The Leibstandarte-SS 'Adolf Hitler' took part in the Berlin victory parade on 19 July 1940. Some participating soldiers were already wearing collar patches without the black/aluminium twisted cord piping, which was officially abolished the following month.*

- 4 September SS-Obersturmführer Fritz Vogt, Staff Reconnaissance, SS-Verfügungsdivision
- September SS-Sturmbannführer Fritz Witt, commander 1st Company, SS-Regiment 'Deutschland'

Many others were decorated with lower grades of the Iron Cross, wound badges and associated combat awards. In September, the Leibstandarte was presented with a new standard by Himmler at its barracks in Metz, and Hitler told them: 'You, who bear my name, will have the honour of leading every German attack'. The Waffen-SS had won its spurs in convincing style.

Germany's success in Western Europe opened up a new reservoir of pro-Nazi Volksdeutsche and Germanic peoples whom the Wehrmacht had no authority to conscript and whom Gottlob Berger, head of the SS Hauptamt, set about recruiting into the Waffen-SS. With the consequent increase in SS numbers, the Leibstandarte was upgraded to brigade strength and a completely new division was authorised, the bulk of its personnel being Nordic volunteers from Flanders, Holland, Norway and Denmark. The leadership of the new division was drawn from existing formations and it totally incorporated the 'Germania' regiment of SS-V. Initially adopting the name SS-Division 'Germania', the new unit was retitled 'Wiking' at the end of 1940 and placed under the command of Felix Steiner. It was to become one of the finest divisions in the SS Order of Battle.

To make up for the loss of the 'Germania' regiment, the SS-Verfügungsdivision was assigned a Totenkopfstandarte and in January 1941 it was renamed SS-Division 'Reich'. The other Totenkopfstandarten were reorganised to play a more active role as independent formations. Two Death's Head regiments, plus artillery and support units, were formed into SS-Kampfgruppe 'Nord', and another Standarte was sent to Norway for occupation duty as SS-Infantry Regiment 9. The five remaining Totenkopfstandarten went to the Waffen-SS training ground at Debica in Poland where they were re-equipped and designated as SS-Infantry Regiments. Finally, the existing Death's Head cavalry units amalgamated to become SS-Kavallerie Regiments 1 and 2.

During the spring of 1941, Germany prepared for the impending invasion of the Soviet Union. When Mussolini's surprise attack on Greece went disastrously wrong and a new anti-German régime seized power in Yugoslavia, Hitler ordered immediate action to secure his southern flank. On 6 April, a Blitzkrieg was unleashed on Yugoslavia and Greece.

SS-Division 'Reich' was in the forefront of the attack and a small assault detachment under SS-Hauptsturmführer Fritz Klingenberg audaciously captured the Yugoslav capital of Belgrade on 13 April. By using a motorboat, Klingenberg and his men were able to slip through the city defences and force its surrender from a confused and bewildered Mayor. In Greece the Leibstandarte was engaged in a series of more hard-fought battles against not only the Greeks but also British and New Zealand troops. After suffering heavy losses at the Klidi Pass, the LAH reconnaissance battalion commanded by SS-Sturmbannführer Kurt Meyer took the strategically crucial Klissura Pass and almost 11,000 prisoners into the bargain. On 20 April, General Tsolakoglu of the Greek III Army Corps surrendered to Sepp Dietrich and a week later Athens fell to the German forces. By the end of the month, the Balkan campaign was effectively over. It had been another victory for the Waffen-SS. Klingenberg, Meyer and Gerd Pleiss, commander of the Leibstandarte's 1st Company which had been most active at Klidi, became the latest recipients of the Knight's Cross. A propaganda film, *'Der Weg Der LAH'*, extolled their exploits.

At dawn on 22 June 1941, Hitler ordered his forces into Russia to begin the epic conflict of ideologies which became a war of extermination and was to change forever the hitherto generally chivalrous character of the Waffen-SS. The rigours of the Eastern Front, encompassing everything from bitterly cold winters to sweltering summers, and from endless steppes and swamps to mountains and forests, brought out the very best, and the very worst, in Hitler's men.

The German deployment for Operation 'Barbarossa' extended from the Baltic to the Black Sea and was organised into three Army Groups designated North, Centre and South. The SS-Totenkopf-Division, the Polizei-Division and Kampfgruppe 'Nord'

Fig 3: *Citation for the Demjansk Shield awarded to SS-Unterscharführer Johann Haselwanter of 2nd Company, Signals Battalion, SS-Totenkopf-Division. It bears the stamped facsimile signature of General Walter Graf Brockdorff-Ahlefeld, commander of the 2nd Armeekorps at Demjansk, who died seven months before the citations for this decoration were distributed in his name.*

FIG 3

Besitzzeugnis

Im Namen des Führers

wurde dem SS- Unterscharführer

Johann Haselwanter

2./SS-Pz.Nachr.Abt. "Totenkopf"

der Demjanskschild verliehen.

K.Gef.St. den 31.12.1943

General der Infanterie

Für die Richtigkeit:

Oberleutnant

21

Plate 21: *Himmler and SS-Brigadeführer Knoblauch reviewing Totenkopf cavalrymen in Russia, July 1941. At this stage in their development, the Waffen-SS Reiterstandarten were mounted on bicycles as often as they were on horses! The officer behind Himmler, wearing a steel helmet, is Hermann Fegelein, later commander of the cavalry division 'Florian Geyer'.*

Plate 22: *The face of the Waffen-SS: troops of the 6th SS-Totenkopf Infantry Regiment operating a captured Czechoslovak ZB53 machine-gun in Russia during the autumn of 1941.*

22

were assigned to Army Group North, SS-Division 'Reich' to Army Group Centre and the Leibstandarte and SS-Division 'Wiking' to Army Group South. The latter two formations particularly impressed their army counterparts by their aggression and skill in attack. 'Reich' was heavily engaged at Minsk, Smolensk and Borodino, where Hausser lost an eye, and the division came within a few kilometres of Moscow at the end of the year. The only real SS failure occurred on the Finnish Front when the second-rate troops of Kampfgruppe 'Nord' were thrown into a mass panic and ignominiously routed on 2 July. The unit had to be withdrawn and completely overhauled, and it was thereafter reinforced with seasoned veterans from the Totenkopf-Division to become SS-Division 'Nord'.

At the end of 1941 the great German offensive came to a halt, totally exhausted. Blitzkrieg techniques had met their match in the vast expanse of the Soviet Union and the stamina and apparently endless manpower reserves of the Red Army. The force of the Russian counter-offensive during the winter of 1941-42 shocked the German Army High Command, which argued for full-scale withdrawals. Hitler overruled the Generals, however, and the Wehrmacht and Waffen-SS had their first opportunity to exhibit their steadfastness in defence.

Plate 23: *SS soldiers lie where they fell, killed in the Soviet counter-offensive which took place during the horrendous winter of 1941-42.* IWM

German troops began to find themselves cut off in isolated 'pockets', the most notable being that at Demjansk which contained six divisions, including 'Totenkopf'. The winter campaign was so harsh, with temperatures regularly falling below -40°C, that a special medal was later authorised for participants. The honour of designing it fell to SS-Unterscharführer Ernst Krause, an artist serving as a war correspondent with the Leibstandarte.

In the spring of 1942 the Germans opened a new offensive in the south, to reach the oil-rich Caucasus region. During the course of the year the Waffen-SS divisions, still suffering from the battles of the previous winter, were withdrawn in turn and refitted with a strong tank component plus assault guns and armoured personnel carriers. In May, the upgraded SS-Division 'Reich' was renamed 'Das Reich', and in September the SS-Kavallerie-Division was activated for anti-partisan duties behind the lines. November saw the Leibstandarte, 'Das Reich', 'Totenkopf' and 'Wiking' officially redesignated as SS-Panzergrenadier Divisions, now equal in terms of equipment to many full panzer divisions of the army. Hitler was increasingly impressed with the combat performance of the SS, and in December ordered the formation of two completely new Waffen-SS divisions, 'Hohenstaufen' and 'Frundsberg'. By the end of the year, Waffen-SS troops in the field numbered around 200,000.

The Soviet offensive of December 1942 proved disastrous for the Germans. All attempts to capture Stalingrad failed and by early 1943 General Paulus's 6th Army was totally isolated and forced to surrender. Other German forces in the Caucasus also faced the grim possibility of being cut off by the speed and depth of the Soviet penetration. Field Marshal von Manstein, commander of Army Group South, managed to withdraw his forces from the Russian trap, however, and sensing that the Soviet thrust had become dangerously over-extended he launched a rapid counter-attack in the Kharkov region. Kharkov was a prestige target, a prewar showcase for Communism, and to spearhead the assault on the city an SS-Panzer-Korps comprising the Leibstandarte, 'Das Reich' and 'Totenkopf' was formed under the overall command of Paul Hausser. For the first time, a substantial body of Waffen-SS troops fought together under their own Generals and the result was a resounding victory. The Soviets were

24

25

Plate 24: *Leibstandarte infantrymen training at their base on the shores of the Sea of Azov, July 1942.*

Plate 25: *A kettle-drummer of the SS-Kavallerie-Division in October 1942. The drum cover was made from black velvet with heavy aluminium wire embroidery, and its design had remained unchanged since 1934.*

thrown into disarray, their 1st Guards Army was destroyed, Kharkov was retaken and the Germans were able to restore order in the south. The SS suffered 12,000 casualties in the process. To Hitler, who was becoming increasingly disillusioned with army failures, it was proof of the capabilities of the Waffen-SS. Decorations were showered upon the victors of Kharkov, and no less than 26 Knight's Crosses, four sets of oakleaves and one set of swords went to the men of the SS-Panzer-Korps. The city's Red Square was renamed 'Platz der Leibstandarte' in honour of Hitler's guards. Moreover, the Führer arranged for his old favourite, Theodor Eicke, who had been killed during the early stages of the offensive, to be buried in the style of the ancient Germanic kings, with all the attendant Pagan ritual.

26

Plate 26: *The 'Sonderkraftfahrzeug' series of half-tracks was widely used by the Waffen-SS in a variety of roles. On 14 March 1943 the Leibstandarte entered Kharkov and a column of SdKfz251s swiftly carried SS panzergrenadiers into the heart of the city.*

Plate 27: *Citation for the Oakleaves and Swords to the Knight's Cross, awarded to Sepp Dietrich after the recapture of Kharkov. The document is signed by Hitler.* West Point Museum

27

IM NAMEN
DES DEUTSCHEN VOLKES
VERLEIHE ICH
DEM SS-OBERGRUPPENFÜHRER
UND GENERAL DER WAFFEN-SS
SEPP DIETRICH
DAS EICHENLAUB MIT SCHWERTERN
ZUM RITTERKREUZ
DES EISERNEN KREUZES
FÜHRERHAUPTQUARTIER
DEN 14. MÄRZ 1943
DER FÜHRER
UND OBERSTE BEFEHLSHABER
DER WEHRMACHT

The period after the German recapture of Kharkov was relatively quiet, as both sides prepared to resume hostilities in the summer. The Soviet salient around Kursk became the focus of events, and when battle commenced on 5 July Hausser's SS-Panzer-Korps, with 340 tanks including Tigers and 195 assault guns, was deployed on the southern flank. The Germans made reasonable progress in the first few days, but the nature of the war had changed and greatly improved Red Army forces held the enemy at bay before successfully counter-attacking. The SS-Panzer-Korps, ultimately reduced to 200 tanks, again fought well, despite being weakened by the removal of the Leibstandarte which was transferred to bolster the German army in Italy following the Allied invasion of Sicily on 10 July.

Kursk was a strategic failure for the Germans. They lost their chance to gain the initiative and from then on were forced to react to Soviet moves. For the rest of 1943, the Germans fell back westwards across the Soviet Union. The three élite SS divisions, now re-designated as full panzer divisions, spent these hard months acting as Hitler's 'fire brigade', being sent from one danger area to another as the situation demanded. The decisiveness with which both 'Das Reich' and 'Totenkopf' threw back Russian assaults earned them repeated praise from those army Generals who were fortunate enough to have them under their command. In November, the Leibstandarte returned to the Eastern Front re-equipped with large numbers of the latest Panther tanks and, together with army panzer divisions, it crushed a Soviet armoured corps in the Ukraine and re-took Zhitomir.

28

Plate 28: *A motorcyclist of the 5th Reconnaissance Company, 'Das Reich', on the Mius Front in August 1943. The twin bar emblem on the front of the sidecar was used as a divisional symbol by 'Das Reich' during the Battle of Kursk, while the Leibstandarte used a single bar and 'Totenkopf' a triple bar. Hausser had devised these temporary formation signs with the intention of confusing Russian intelligence in the lead-up to Kursk.*

29

30

Plate 29: *Totenkopf personnel watching Russian positions on the southern sector of the Eastern Front, October 1943. The man with the binoculars wears the recently introduced Einheitsfeldmütze, while the panzer officer still sports his black version of the M40 schiffchen with aluminium piping. Note also the unofficial sheepskin overjacket and fur cap used by the soldier on the right.*

Plate 30: *A soldier of the Belgian SS Assault Brigade 'Wallonien' under shellfire at Cherkassy, December 1943.*

While the Waffen-SS was locked in battle on the Eastern Front, Hitler continued to authorise the formation of new SS divisions. Manpower shortages had become so acute that a programme was set up during 1943 to encourage the voluntary enlistment of 17 year olds, boys who would not have been subject to normal Wehrmacht conscription until 1946. The SS saw this as a golden opportunity to build up its own forces, since young men who could be persuaded to volunteer for the Waffen-SS before reaching their 20th year, the normal age for conscript service, usually had their preference for that branch of the fighting forces respected. Negotiations between Himmler and the Reichsjugendführer, Artur Axmann, took place as a result of which it was decided to raise an entirely new Waffen-SS division from Hitler Youths who had completed their paramilitary training. By mid-summer, the required number of 10,000 volunteers had been mustered, together with a cadre of 180 officers and 800 experienced NCOs seconded from the Leibstandarte, 'Das Reich' and 'Totenkopf', as well as from various army units. In October, the division was officially named 'Hitlerjugend' and command was given to Fritz Witt.

The German position on the Eastern Front underwent a drastic deterioration when the Soviets launched a massive offensive in the Ukraine on 14 December 1943. The battle lasted for four months and culminated in the expulsion of the German forces from the south. The speed of the Soviet advance led to the encirclement of large numbers of German troops. 'Wiking', now under the command of SS-Gruppenführer Herbert Gille, and Léon Degrelle's Belgian SS Brigade 'Wallonien' were caught in the Korsun-Cherkassy Pocket in a scene reminiscent of Stalingrad, but managed to smash their way out, suffering 60 per cent casualties in the process. Degrelle received the Knight's Cross, and Gille the swords, for this action. In a similar engagement, the Leibstandarte and elements of 'Das Reich' were trapped around Kamenets Podolsky and had to be rescued by 'Hohenstaufen' and 'Frundsberg'. Worn down and exhausted, the Waffen-SS formations were now increasingly unable to stem the advancing Russian tide.

31

Plate 31: *SS-Gruppenführer Herbert-Otto Gille, who won the Knight's Cross with Oakleaves and Swords for his leadership of the 'Wiking' division at Cherkassy. The lower neck decoration is the Finnish Freedom Cross.*

In the spring of 1944, the battered Leibstandarte and 'Das Reich' battle groups were sent westwards to refit and prepare for the expected Anglo-American invasion. The former went to Belgium while the latter went to southern France. They were joined by 'Hitlerjugend' and the 'Götz von Berlichingen' division, which had been formed in France a few months earlier. 'Hohenstaufen' and 'Frundsberg' had relocated in Poland in anticipation of another Soviet attack, along with the emaciated 'Wiking', while the long-suffering 'Totenkopf' remained in front-line service in the east.

When the Normandy landings struck on 6 June, 'Hitlerjugend' was the first SS formation to engage the enemy. The ferocity of the SS assault shocked the Allies, but their command of the air prevented proper deployment of the division and the attack ground to a halt. Two months of bloody fighting ensued. The Leibstandarte and 'Hitlerjugend' were grouped together to form I.SS-Panzer-Korps under Sepp Dietrich, and were immediately assigned the task of defending key positions around Caen. 'Götz von Berlichingen' was hindered by constant air attacks on its journey north from its base in the Loire valley, and did not reach the invasion front until 11 June. 'Das Reich', travelling from Gascony, took even longer, being subjected to a series of ambushes carried out by the French Resistance. Frustrated at the consequent delays and loss of life the division wreaked havoc upon the local population whom it suspected of sheltering the partisans. The village of Oradour-sur-Glane was systematically destroyed and 640 of its inhabitants were shot, and the little town of Tulle was also devastated. 'Das Reich' eventually reached its positions north of St Lô at the end of June, to join up with Willi Bittrich's II.SS-Panzer-Korps, comprising 'Hohenstaufen' and 'Frundsberg', which had been hurriedly transferred from the east.

Throughout July the six SS divisions struggled ceaselessly to contain the Allies in their beachhead, taking a heavy toll of British and American armour. In one notable engagement, SS-Obersturmführer Michael Wittmann and his Leibstandarte Tiger crew destroyed 21 British tanks and 28 other armoured vehicles in a single hour. However, the Germans were overtaken by the sheer weight of Allied numbers and were frequently reduced to operating as *ad hoc* battle groups. By the middle of August, 19 German army divisions had become trapped around Falaise and only determined efforts by 'Das Reich', 'Hitlerjugend' and 'Hohenstaufen' kept open a gap long enough for them to escape. Increasingly, while ordinary German soldiers were prepared to surrender to the Allies, it was left to the SS to fight on.

Meanwhile, in the east, the Red Army had struck again on 13 July and ripped Army Group Centre apart. Once more, the

32

Plate 32: *In a scene reminiscent of World War I, an SS-Schütze shelters in his trench dugout on the Eastern Front, spring 1944.*

Plate 33: *Volunteers for the 'Hitlerjugend' division swear an oath of loyalty before the Sig-runes, flanked by Hitler Youth flags, in 1944. The smart M36 uniform of the helmeted officer contrasts sharply with the more basic M43 dress worn by the recruits.*

SS panzer divisions were thrown into the breach. 'Wiking' and 'Totenkopf', grouped together as IV.SS-Panzer-Korps under Herbert Gille, repulsed the Soviet attack on Warsaw during August, while in the Balkans the backbone of the German defence was provided by 'Prinz Eugen', 'Handschar' and other nominally second-grade formations of SS-Obergruppenführer Artur Phleps' V.SS-Gebirgs-Korps, which had been withdrawn from their usual anti-partisan duties.

In September, the British airborne assault on Arnhem was countered and defeated by 'Hohenstaufen ' and 'Frundsberg' in a battle noted for the mutual respect held by each side for the fighting abilities and fair play of the other. This victory, and the general slowing down of the Allied advance across France due to over-extended supply and communications lines, persuaded Hitler to launch a major offensive in the west, in an attempt to

Plate 34: *A 'Hitlerjugend' MG42 team alongside a Panther tank in Normandy, June 1944. All wear standard helmet covers and smocks, with baggy Italian-pattern camouflage trousers.*

repeat the successes of 1940. Two panzer armies were assembled to spearhead the attack, the 5th Panzer Army under General Hasso von Manteuffel, and the 6th SS-Panzer Army, the larger of the two forces, under Sepp Dietrich. The nucleus of the latter army comprised the Leibstandarte, 'Das Reich', 'Hohenstaufen' and 'Hitlerjugend', now equipped with some of the latest King Tiger tanks. On 16 December the offensive began in the Ardennes, but the hilly and wooded terrain naturally favoured defensive action and after only five days the German advance ground to a halt. SS frustration again translated itself into the committing of atrocities, this time the massacre of 70 American prisoners by men of Joachim Peiper's battle group at Malmédy. A subsidiary offensive in Alsace, led by 'Götz von Berlichingen', also came to nothing and the division ended up trapped in Metz. With a virtual stalemate in the west, Hitler pulled his SS divisions out and sent them eastwards, where the situation had once more become desperate.

On 12 January 1945, a great Soviet offensive was launched across Poland in preparation for the final assault on Berlin. Even so, Hitler's main concern was to safeguard the tenuous hold he still maintained over the Hungarian oilfields. The SS cavalry divisions 'Florian Geyer' and 'Maria Theresa' were besieged in Budapest, and in an effort to relieve them 'Totenkopf' and 'Wiking' were transferred from their key positions on the German-Polish border. A month-long battle failed to save the city, however, and it fell to the Russians on 13 February with only 785 German soldiers escaping from the original garrison of 50,000 men. The 6th SS-Panzer Army was immediately moved in from the west and on 6 March a German counter-attack began. It was conducted by the largest aggregation of Waffen-SS forces ever witnessed during the war, comprising the Leibstandarte, 'Das Reich', 'Totenkopf', 'Wiking', 'Hohenstaufen', 'Hitlerjugend' and 'Reichsführer-SS', the latter having been transferred from northern Italy. At first the SS did well, but there were insufficient back-up resources and by mid-March their advance had been halted.

The failure of the Waffen-SS in Hungary, following on from the collapse of the Ardennes offensive, had a devastating psychological effect on Hitler who had come to expect the impossible from them, and he openly accused Dietrich and his subordinates of betrayal. Despite that, SS troops carried on fighting as loyally as ever as they slowly retreated into Germany, bowed under the weight of superior Allied numbers and equipment. By now, thousands of 'grounded' Luftwaffe personnel and 'beached' sailors from the Kriegsmarine had been pressed into an infantry role alongside the Waffen-SS. During the last week in April, when Soviet forces broke into Berlin, Felix Steiner led a battle group of hard-core Waffen-SS including elements of the 'Polizei', 'Frundsberg', 'Nordland', 'Wallonien', 'Charlemagne', and 'Nederland' divisions, as well as some 600 men from Himmler's personal escort battalion, in a life and death struggle to defend the Führerbunker. However, most other SS units had by then accepted the reality of

Plate 35: *Theodor Wisch, one of the original 120 members of the SS Stabswache 'Berlin' in March 1933, succeeded Sepp Dietrich as commander of the Leibstandarte-SS 'Adolf Hitler' and led the division during the Normandy battles of June-August 1944. He was badly wounded on 20 August and spent the rest of the war 'driving a desk' on attachment to the SS Führungshauptamt.*

35

the situation and were pushing westwards to surrender to the Anglo-American Allies, rather than risk capture by the Russians.

It is estimated that some 180,000 Waffen-SS soldiers were killed in action during World War 2, with about 400,000 wounded and a further 70,000 listed 'missing'. The entire establishment of the élite divisions, Leibstandarte, 'Das Reich' and 'Totenkopf' were casualties several times over, with only a few battle-hardened veterans surviving to train the continual injections of young Germans and Volksdeutsche fed in as replacements via the divisional training battalions. A close comparison between the number of men recorded killed, wounded or missing in the 'Totenkopf' division (60,000) and 'Wiking' division (19,000) gives a startlingly different loss ratio. Since both divisions served for the most part alongside each other, the only reason for such horrendous losses must have been the mishandling, or rough handling, of 'Totenkopf' troops by their commanders. Certainly, Eicke and his successors were not renowned as humanitarians and it is known that 'Totenkopf' had more requests for 'transfers out' than any other Waffen-SS division. A large proportion of the men who volunteered for service in the SS paratroop forces were 'Totenkopf' transferees, and it was widely recognised that the paratroop battalion was virtually a suicide squad. The fact that many hardened soldiers chose to escape from 'Totenkopf' by signing up with the paras gives an indication of the severity and long-term nature of the suffering which 'Totenkopf' troops had to endure.

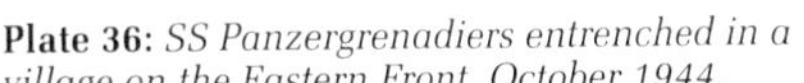

Plate 36: *SS Panzergrenadiers entrenched in a village on the Eastern Front, October 1944.*

36

37

Plate 37: *Soldiers of Dietrich's 6th SS-Panzer army take a Belgian village during the Ardennes offensive, December 1944. An American armoured vehicle is just visible through the smoke.*

By 1944-45, SS soldiers were normally in their late teens and the average age of a Waffen-SS junior officer was 20 with a life expectancy of two months at the front. Moreover, it was not uncommon for divisional commanders to be in their early 30s, men like Kraas, Kumm, Meyer, Mohnke, Wisch and Witt who had joined the SS-VT around 1934 and progressed through the ranks. The combination of youthful enthusiasm, political indoctrination and hard-bitten experience was a winning one, and goes a long way to explaining how a division such as 'Hitlerjugend' could suffer 60 per cent casualties over a four-week period in 1944 and yet still retain its aggressive spirit, thereby gaining for the entire Waffen-SS the admiration of friend and foe alike.

After the war, the blood sacrifices of the Waffen-SS and their genuine services to the German nation were quickly forgotten in the rush towards 'de-Nazification'. Former SS soldiers were declared ex-members of a criminal organisation and were excluded from any entitlement to the disability pensions and other benefits paid out to those who had served with the Wehrmacht. As a result, the Welfare Association of Former Soldiers of the Waffen-SS (Hilfsgemeinschaft auf Gegenseitigkeit der Soldaten der ehemal Waffen-SS, or HIAG) was set up to campaign for their rights, and it was moderately successful.

Gradually, former members of the Waffen-SS were accorded the respect which they richly deserved. By 1966, the year in which Sepp Dietrich, Georg Keppler, Herbert Gille and Felix Steiner all died, public opinion had shifted sufficiently to permit large attendances at their funerals.

Plate 38: *An SS motorcycle registration plate which was 'liberated' by a British serviceman at the end of the war.*

Himmler always intended that the SS should develop as a Germanic, rather than a German, organisation and he aimed to attract all the 'best Nordic blood of Europe' into it so that never again would the Germanic peoples come into mutual conflict. To that end, small numbers of non-Germans were admitted to the Allgemeine-SS and SS-Verfügungstruppe even before the war, including at least one soldier of dual German/British nationality who served with the SS-VT Standarte 'Deutschland'. Prior to 1939, every candidate for entry into any branch of the SS had to furnish documentary proof of Aryan descent to the SS Rasse- und Siedlungshauptamt (RuSHA) which was the only competent authority for checking genealogical records and deciding on the racial suitability of the person concerned. With the rapid expansion of the Waffen-SS after 1940, however, the racial rule became something of a dead letter for its 750,000 rank and file. During the war, the hard-pressed RuSHA authorities were content to accept a signed declaration of Aryan descent from enlisted German and West European Waffen-SS men, which could be investigated later when necessity demanded or when the opportunity presented itself.

With the German conquest of Western Europe, the door to a huge pool of manpower which the Wehrmacht had no authority to conscript was opened to Berger's recruiting officers. Large numbers of pro-Germans, anti-Bolsheviks, members of local pseudo-Nazi political parties, adventurers and simple opportunists were only too eager to throw in their lot with the winning side. The first complete unit of foreign volunteers to be raised by the SS was the Standarte 'Nordland', from Norwegians and Danes. It was soon joined by the Standarte 'Westland', comprising Dutchmen and Flemings, and in December 1940 these two formations combined with the SS-VT Standarte 'Germania' to become SS-Division 'Wiking', a truly European force. The main impetus to the recruiting of further so-called 'foreign legions' was the impending invasion of the Soviet Union, and in order to attract sufficient numbers of these troops the Germans reluctantly accepted the need to co-operate with the pro-Nazi political parties in each country, and that the new units would have to retain some of their own national characteristics. The idea of national legions was quickly extended from the Germanic countries to those ideologically sympathetic to Germany, like Croatia. However, during the early stages of the war at least, Himmler was not prepared to accept racially dubious volunteers into the SS and so the eastern legions, like the French, Walloon Belgians and Spaniards, were assigned to the army.

During 1940-41, the SS-sponsored legions 'Flandern', 'Niederlande', 'Norwegen' and 'Freikorps Danmark' were raised. Their troops were distinguished from those in the German SS proper by special

Plate 39: *Himmler and Quisling inspecting Norwegian volunteers for the SS-Standarte 'Nordland', 9 February 1941.*

Plate 40: *The 'Black Lion of Flanders' on a yellow shield, worn by members of the Flemish Legion and the 'Langemarck' assault brigade.*

national badges and by their oath, which committed them solely to the war against Communism. The legions were categorised as being 'attached to' rather than 'part of' the Waffen-SS, and were designated by the new title of 'Freiwilligen' or 'Volunteer' units. The recruitment programme soon ran into difficulties, however, when the legionaries found that many of their German colleagues held them in low regard. Despite promises of free land in the conquered east for all victorious SS soldiers, morale plummeted, particularly when 'Flandern' was decimated in Russia early in 1942 and had to be disbanded. The other three legions were reinforced and, at the end of 1942, amalgamated to form the 'Nordland' division. A year later the Dutch contingent was sufficiently strong to be removed and given the status of an independent brigade, which ultimately developed into the 'Nederland' division. Both 'Nordland' and 'Nederland' fought well on the Eastern Front, particularly in defence of the Baltic States, and together with the rest of Felix Steiner's III (Germanisches) SS-Panzer-Korps they took part in the celebrated 'Battle of the European SS' at Narva in July 1944 before being destroyed in the final struggle for Berlin the following year. Other western SS formations of note included the 'Wallonien' division, which was transferred from the army as a brigade in 1943 and fought with distinction under the Belgian fascist leader Léon Degrelle, and the French 'Charlemagne' division, again transferred from the army, which was one of the most redoubtable defenders of Berlin. A 58-strong 'British Free Corps' was drawn from former British Union of Fascists (BUF) members and other disaffected individuals in British POW camps, but was of propaganda value only.

Despite the good fighting reputation quickly gained by the western volunteers, they were simply too few in number to meet SS requirements for replacing battle casualties and so Berger turned to the Volksdeutsche, or racial Germans, scattered throughout central and eastern Europe. They were the descendants of many generations of Germans who had moved eastwards since the Middle Ages in search of new lands and livelihoods, and who had settled across an enormous region from the Baltic States to the Caucasus. In just three countries, Romania, Hungary and Yugoslavia, it was estimated that there were some 1,500,000 Volksdeutsche in 1939 and this was clearly a rich source of potential manpower. Recruitment of Romanian Volksdeutsche began as early as the spring of 1940, but a sudden influx of volunteers from Yugoslavia after the invasion of April 1941 led Berger to suggest to Himmler the formation of an entire division of Yugoslav Volksdeutsche. The result was the raising in the summer of 1942 of the SS-Gebirgs Division 'Prinz Eugen', designed for anti-partisan duties against Tito's resistance movement. Later that year, faced with an ever-worsening manpower crisis, the SS was given authorisation to formally conscript the Volksdeutsche, who fell without the remit of the Wehrmacht as they were not German nationals. In that way, an impressive numerical level of

Fig 4: *Recruiting poster for the Norwegian Legion, dating from 1941. It reads: 'With the Waffen-SS and the Norwegian Legion against the common enemy – against Bolshevism'.*

FIG 4

MED WAFFEN-SS OG
DEN NORSKE LEGION
MOT DEN FELLES FIENDE....
MOT BOLSJEVISMEN

FIG 5

Vlamingen op!
MELDT U AAN : bij de WAFFEN-SS of bij
het VRIJWILLIGERSLEGIOEN VLAANDEREN
ERSATZKOMMANDO FLANDERN DER WAFFEN - SS - ANTWERPEN, KONINGIN ELISABETHLEI, 22

Fig 5: *Recruiting poster for the Flemish Legion, declaring 'Flemings Rise Up!'. It depicts a Waffen-SS soldier as the direct descendant of a national hero, a theme common to recruiting drives in the Germanic countries.*

recruitment was maintained, but many of the conscripts were poor in quality and consequently Volksdeutsche units tended to be second rate. They soon earned for themselves the reputation of being specialists in perpetrating massacres against civilian populations and other soft targets. The associated policy of recruiting Croatian and Albanian Muslims into the 'Handschar', 'Kama' and 'Skanderbeg' divisions, to take on the Christian Serbs from whom many of Tito's partisans were drawn, was a total disaster and all three divisions had to be disbanded in order to free their German officers and NCOs to fight elsewhere.

In the Soviet Union, the Germans made better use of local nationalist groups opposed to Stalin's government, successfully persuading large numbers of the native population to enrol in the Schutzmannschaft or auxiliary police force for counter-guerrilla operations. The breakthrough for the Waffen-SS recruiters came in April 1943, when no less than 100,000 Ukrainians volunteered for a new SS division, of whom 30,000 were duly accepted. Over 80 per cent of them were killed the following year when the Ukrainian division was trapped in the Brody-Tarnow pocket.

In the summer of 1944, after the failed July bomb plot against Hitler, Himmler was given unprecedented military powers as Chief of the Replacement Army and he took the opportunity to increase his personal status still further by transferring many Armenian, Baltic, Caucasian, Cossack, Georgian and Turkestani volunteers from the hastily-mustered foreign legions of the German army into the Waffen-SS. However, while the wide range of nationalities involved undoubtedly had some propaganda value, the actual performance of the eastern troops in combat left much to be desired. The Baltic SS divisions, grouped together under SS-Obergruppenführer Walter Krüger as VI. Waffen-Armeekorps der SS, lived up to modest expectations and were particularly ferocious when defending their homelands, but the remainder were poor at best and at worst a complete rabble. Himmler regarded them merely as racially inferior auxiliaries, in effect expendable cannon-fodder. They were never considered for SS membership proper, and were prohibited from sporting the SS runes. Although they wore a sort of diluted SS uniform for convenience sake, they had their own series of distinctive badges so that there would be absolutely no possibility of their being mistaken for 'real' SS men. Not surprisingly, the loyalty of the easterners was always in question and their horrific behaviour when set loose amongst the civilian population of Poland during

Plate 41: *Himmler inspecting Bosnian Muslims of the 'Handschar' artillery regiment being trained in the use of a Pak 38 anti-tank gun at Neuhammer in Silesia, October 1943.*

41

42

Plate 42: *In May 1944, Haj Amin al-Husaini, the self-styled Grand Mufti of Jerusalem and spiritual leader of Bosnia's Muslims, reviewed troops of the 'Handschar' division who were kitted out with their distinctive field-grey fez.*

43

the Warsaw Uprising of autumn 1944 led to frequent demands for their withdrawal, even from other SS commanders. Several units had to be disbanded and some of their leaders were tried by SS courts martial and executed for looting and other excesses.

Non-German nationals ultimately made up the greater part (57 per cent) of the Waffen-SS. It is estimated that 400,000 Reich Germans served in the Waffen-SS during the war as opposed to 137,000 pure West Europeans, 200,000 pure East Europeans and 185,000 Volksdeutsche, the latter group including the sons of German ancestors who had emigrated overseas during the 19th and early 20th centuries. A detailed breakdown of non-Germans by nationality is shown in the table below.

Plate 43: *SS-Obergruppenführer Artur Phleps, founder of the 'Prinz Eugen' division and commander of the V. SS-Gebirgs-Korps in 1944. Phleps was a racial German from Romania who had served on the General Staff of the Imperial Austro-Hungarian army during World War 1 and later as an instructor at the Bucharest Military Academy. Unlike most of his Volksdeutsche subordinates, Phleps was granted full SS membership as indicated by the runes worn below the left breast pocket. He was captured and subsequently killed by Russian soldiers on 21 September 1944.*

44

Plate 44: *The Flemish SS-Sturmmann Richard 'Remi' Schrijnen of 3rd Company, SS-Freiwilligen Sturmbrigade 'Langemarck', being paraded before his fellow soldiers near Prague after receiving the Knight's Cross on 21 September 1944. He is accompanied by Konrad Schellong, the brigade commander, and adjutant Willy Teichert.*

Volksdeutsche (by country of origin)	
Hungary	80,000
Czechoslovakia	45,000
Croatia	25,000
Western Europe	16,000
Romania	8,000
Poland	5,000
Serbia	5,000
Scandinavia	775
Soviet Union	100
France	84
Great Britain	10
USA	5
Brazil	4
China	3
South West Africa	3
South East Africa	2
South America	2
Spain	2
Palestine	2
Japan	2
Sumatra	2
Mexico	1
Australia	1
India	1
New Guinea	1

West Europeans		***East Europeans***	
Dutch	50,000	Cossacks	50,000
Flemings	23,000	Latvians	35,000
Italians	20,000	Ukrainians	30,000
Walloons	15,000	Estonians	20,000
Danes	11,000	Croatians	20,000
French	8,000	Serbians	15,000
Norwegians	6,000	Byelorussians	12,000
Spaniards/Swiss/ Swedes/ Luxembourgers/ British (total)	4,000	Turkestanis	8,000
		Romanians	5,000
		Albanians	3,000
		Bulgarians	1,000
		Finns	1,000

45

Plate 45: *The abandoned Waffen-SS recruiting office at Calais, 12 October 1944. Over 8,000 Frenchmen joined the Waffen-SS during World War 2.*

Plate 46: *Léon Degrelle and men of his Walloon division in Pomerania, 9 March 1945. Degrelle wears the Close Combat Clasp in Gold and his unique 'Wallonien' cuff title hand-embroidered in Gothic script. Note also the single-button late war Einheitsfeldmützen worn by the men standing behind him. The SS-Unterscharführer in the foreground is a Frenchman, Jean Lejeune.*

Although given suitably heroic names from an early date, Waffen-SS divisions were not numbered until 15 November 1943. Unit titles and designations were frequently altered, either to acknowledge a change in status or, particularly later in the war, to camouflage a formation's true identity and confuse enemy intelligence. The 'Das Reich' division was a typical example and had its nomenclature altered no less than 11 times, as follows:

September 1939	Panzerverband Ostpreussen/Panzer Division 'Kempf'
10.10.39	SS-Verfügungstruppe-Division (Motorised)
4.4.40	SS-Verfügungsdivision
1.12.40	SS-Division 'Deutschland'
28.1.41	SS-Division (Motorised) 'Reich'
May 1942	SS-Division (Motorised) 'Das Reich'/Kampfgruppe 'Ostendorff'
14.11.42	SS-Panzergrenadier Division 'Das Reich'

Fig 6: *A large number of spurious Waffen-SS tactical signs have appeared in various books over the years. Those symbols illustrated here are the only ones which have been confirmed by photographic or documentary evidence as having been painted on the vehicles of the following divisions during World War 2:*

A Leibstandarte-SS 'Adolf Hitler'
B 'Das Reich'
C SS-Totenkopf-Division
D SS-Polizei-Division (1941-43)
E SS-Polizei-Division (1944-45)
F 'Wiking'
G 'Nord' (1944-45)
H 'Prinz Eugen'
I 'Florian Geyer'
J 'Hohenstaufen'
K 'Frundsberg'
L 'Frundsberg' (panzer units only)
M 'Nordland' (1943)
N 'Nordland' (1944-45)
O 'Hitlerjugend'
P 'Handschar' (the 'G' stood for 'Gebirge')
Q 14th Division
R 'Reichsführer-SS'
S 'Reichsführer-SS' (carried over from unofficial use by the Sturmbrigade RfSS)
T 'Götz von Berlichingen'

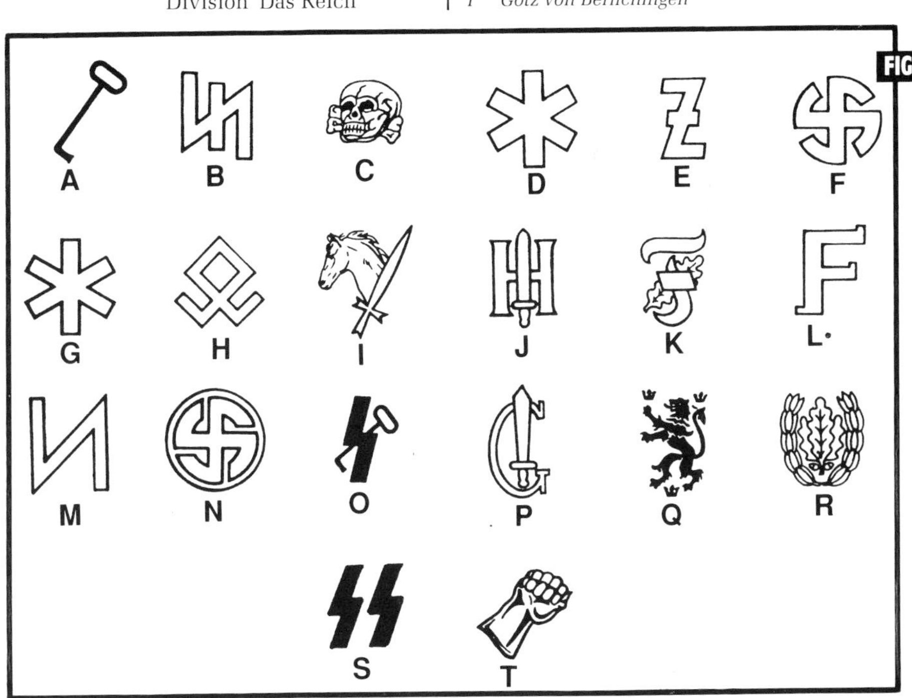

47

Plate 47: *A Leibstandarte motorcycle combination moves through a burning Russian town, July 1941. The divisional emblem of a skeleton key or 'Dietrich', clearly a pun on the name of the LAH commander, can be seen on the rear of the sidecar.*

September	Panzerverband
15.11.43	2nd SS-Panzer Division 'Das Reich'
24.2.45	Ausbildungsgruppe 'Nord'

Divisions staffed by Germans were known as 'SS-Division', while those comprising mainly Volksdeutsche or Germanic personnel, whether volunteers or conscripts, were called 'SS-Freiwilligen Division'. Units composed primarily of East Europeans or Russians came into the category of 'Waffen Division der SS', a term of inferiority which denoted attachment to, rather than actual membership of, the Waffen-SS.

The following table lists all the Waffen-SS divisions which had been mustered, at least on paper, by 1945. Most divisions numbered above 20 were merely upgraded regiments, or even battalions, flung together in a hurry and given grandiose titles. The number of Knight's Crosses awarded is a good indication of the effectiveness and battle experience of each division.

Title	*Granted Divisional Status*	*Primary Composition*	*Knight's Crosses Awarded*
1st SS-Panzer Division Leibstandarte-SS 'Adolf Hitler'	1940	German volunteers with Hitler's SS bodyguard regiment as the nucleus	58
2nd SS-Panzer Division 'Das Reich'	1939	German volunteers with the SS-Verfügungstruppe as the nucleus	69
3rd SS-Panzer Division 'Totenkopf'	1939	German volunteers with the SS-Totenkopfverbände as the nucleus	47
4th SS-Polizei Panzergrenadier Division	1939	German Police transferees	25
5th SS-Panzer Division 'Wiking'	1940	German/West European volunteers	55
6th SS-Gebirgs Division 'Nord'	1940	German volunteers with Totenkopf regiments as the nucleus	4
7th SS-Freiwilligen Gebirgs Division 'Prinz Eugen'	1942	Yugoslavian Volksdeutsche volunteers	6
8th SS-Kavallerie Division 'Florian Geyer'	1942	German volunteers with SS-Kavallerie regiments as the nucleus	22
9th SS-Panzer Division 'Hohenstaufen'	1943	German volunteers and conscripts	12

Title	*Granted Divisional Status*	*Primary Composition*	*Knight's Crosses Awarded*
10th SS-Panzer Division 'Frundsberg'	1943	German volunteers and conscripts	13
11th SS-Freiwilligen Panzergrenadier Division 'Nordland'	1943	West European volunteers many from the disbanded SS foreign legions 'Niederlande', 'Norwegen', and 'Freikorps Danmark'	25
12th SS-Panzer Division 'Hitlerjugend'	1943	German Hitler Youth volunteers	14
13th Waffen Gebirgs Division der SS 'Handschar'	1943	Yugoslavian Muslim volunteers	4
14th Waffen Grenadier Division der SS	1943	Ukrainian volunteers	1
15th Waffen Grenadier Division der SS	1943	Latvian volunteers, many transferring from the Schutzmannschaft and Police Rifle Regiments	3
16th SS-Panzergrenadier Division 'Reichsführer-SS'	1943	German/Volksdeutsche volunteers and conscripts, with Himmler's escort battalion as the nucleus	1
17th SS-Panzergrenadier Division 'Götz von Berlichingen'	1943	German/Volksdeutsche volunteers and conscripts	4
18th SS-Freiwilligen Panzergrenadier Division 'Horst Wessel'	1944	Hungarian Volksdeutsche volunteers and conscripts	2
19th Waffen Grenadier Division der SS	1944	Latvian volunteers, many transferring from the Schutzmannschaft and Police Rifle Regiments	12
20th Waffen Grenadier Division der SS	1944	Estonian volunteers, many transferring from the Schutzmannschaft and Police Rifle Regiments	5
21st Waffen Gebirgs Division der SS 'Skanderbeg'	1944	Albanian Muslim volunteers	0
22nd SS-Freiwilligen Kavallerie Division 'Maria Theresa'	1944	German/Hungarian Volksdeutsche volunteers and conscripts	6
23rd Waffen Gebirgs Division der SS 'Kama' (disbanded late 1944 and number '23' given to next division)	1944	Yugoslavian Muslim volunteers	0
23rd SS-Freiwilligen Panzergrenadier Division 'Nederland'	1944	Dutch volunteers, many formerly of the SS foreign legion 'Niederlande'	19
24th Waffen Gebirgs Division der SS	1944	Italian Fascist volunteers	0
25th Waffen Grenadier Division der SS 'Hunyadi'	1944	Hungarian volunteers	0
26th Waffen Grenadier Division der SS	1945	Hungarian volunteers	0

Title	*Granted Divisional Status*	*Primary Composition*	*Knight's Crosses Awarded*
27th SS-Freiwilligen Grenadier Division 'Langemarck'	1945	Flemish volunteers, many formerly of the SS foreign legion 'Flandern'	1
28th SS-Freiwilligen Grenadier Division 'Wallonien'	1945	Walloon volunteers, many formerly of the German army's Wallonische Legion	3
29th Waffen Grenadier Division der SS (disbanded late 1944 and number '29' given to next division)	1944	Russian convict volunteers	0
29th Waffen Grenadier Division der SS	1945	Italian Fascist volunteers	0
30th Waffen Grenadier Division der SS	1945	Russian volunteers, many transferring from the Schutzmannschaft and Police Rifle Regiments	0
31st SS-Freiwilligen Grenadier Division	1945	Czechoslovak Volksdeutsche volunteers and conscripts	0
32nd SS-Freiwilligen Grenadier Division '30 Januar'	1945	German conscripts and SS training school personnel/Volksdeutsche volunteers and conscripts	0
33rd Waffen Kavallerie Division der SS (destroyed early 1945, and number '33' given to next division)	1945	Hungarian volunteers	0
33rd Waffen Grenadier Division der SS 'Charlemagne'	1945	French volunteers, many formerly of the German army's Französisches Legion or LVF	2
34th SS-Freiwilligen Grenadier Division 'Landstorm Nederland'	1945	Dutch volunteers, many formerly of the Landwacht Nederland	3
35th SS-Polizei Grenadier Division	1945	German Police transferees	0
36th Waffen Grenadier Division der SS	1945	German/East European volunteers, including a large number of convicted criminals from the Dirlewanger Brigade, a terror unit used against civilians	1
37th SS-Freiwilligen Kavallerie Division 'Lützow'	1945	Hungarian Volksdeutsche conscripts and remnants of the 'Florian Geyer' and 'Maria Theresa' divisions	0
38th SS-Grenadier Division 'Nibelungen'	1945	German volunteers, conscripts and SS training school personnel	0

In stark contrast to the Imperial Army, promotion in the Waffen-SS depended upon personal commitment and military effectiveness, not class or education. Consequently, the SS cadet schools at Bad Tölz and Braunschweig consciously offered something which those of the Wehrmacht never did, an officer's career for men without a middle- or upper-class background or formal educational qualifications.

The Waffen-SS always encouraged self-discipline and mutual respect rather than a brutally enforced discipline, and its general working atmosphere was more relaxed than that of the army, the relationship between officers and men being less formal. Officers were termed 'Führer' or 'leaders', not 'Offiziere' which had class connotations. On duty, the old military rank prefix, 'Herr', implying superiority and dominance was strictly forbidden and even the lowliest SS-Schütze would address his Colonel as 'Standartenführer', not 'Herr Standartenführer'. Off duty, junior ranks referred to their seniors as 'Kamerad' (Comrade), or 'Parteigenosse' (Party Colleague) if both were members of the NSDAP.

Any Allgemeine-SS officer who joined the Waffen-SS during the war retained his Allgemeine-SS position and rank, but usually received a lower Waffen-SS rank, often in a reserve capacity, until such time as he had gained sufficient military experience to warrant promotion. Thereafter, any promotion he received in the Waffen-SS resulted in a simultaneous and level upgrading of his Allgemeine-SS rank. Promotion to SS-Gruppenführer and above was decided by Hitler himself, in his technical capacity as Commander-in-Chief of the entire SS, while promotion to all other officer ranks was granted by Himmler upon the recommendation of the SS Personalhauptamt, which in turn acted upon the nominations of unit commanders.

The wartime Waffen-SS officer corps, as recognised by the SS hierarchy, consisted almost entirely of German nationals who held all of the most senior posts. The

Plate 48: *LAH, SS-VT and SS-TV officers on parade outside the Führer Building in Munich, 9 November 1938. Note the aluminium wire aiguillettes and brocade belts worn by commissioned ranks on ceremonial occasions. Most of these men have been issued with the M35 steel helmet, although a few still retain the traditional M16/18 pattern.*

48

Lfde. Nr.	Name, Vorname	Degen/Ring	Dienststellung	Partei-Nr.	SS-Nr.	Geburts-datum	Schule, Jahrgang	Ober-sturm-bann-führer
	SS-Obersturmbannführer:							
3983	Rausch Günter, II I		RSi-Hauptamt	224 360	17 852	19. 5. 09	T 34	9. 11. 42
3984	Neumann Hans,		1. SS-Pz. Div. »LSSAH«	266 400	9 925	4. 8. 10	T 34	30. 1. 43
3985	Schultz Siegfried, I		2. SS-Pz. Div. »DR«	291 207	36 006	4. 12. 09	T 34	20. 4. 43
3986	Stange Martin, I		Kdr. Art. Rgt. 16. SS-Pz. Gr. Div. »RF SS«	*2 731 039*	117 498	30. 3. 10	T 34	9. 11. 43
3987	Zollhöfer Emil, I		Kdr. 19. Rgt. 9. SS-Pz. Div. »H«	917 208	28 501	20. 9. 11	T 35	9. 11. 43
3988	Grensing Erich, I I		1. SS-Pz. Div. »LSSAH«	985 826	35 564	18. 8. 10	B 35	9. 11. 43
3989	Schönfelder Manfred, I		IV. SS-Pz. Korps	1 135 901	59 781	18. 3. 12	T 35	9. 11. 43
3990	Kempin Hans, I I		Kdr. SS-Pz.Gr.Sch.	382 076	51 240	7. 6. 13	T 34	1. 12. 43
3991	Klingenberg Fritz, I II		Kdr. SS-J.Sch. Tölz	851 328	51 487	17. 12. 12	T 34	21. 12. 43
3992	Daufeldt Hans		RSi-Hauptamt	753 151	36 167	20. 1. 08	T 34	30. 1. 44
3993	Weidenhaupt Wilhelm, I		1. SS-Pz. Div. »LSSAH«	1 163 235	45 947	11. 3. 12	T 34	30. 1. 44
3995	Lehmann Rudolf, I		1. SS-Pz. Div. »LSSAH«	*3 143 188*	111 883	30. 1. 14	T 35	30. 1. 44
3996	Keller Baldur, I		V. SS-Geb. Korps	—	111 594	26. 4. 12	B 35	30. 1. 44

3999	Harzer Walter, I		9. SS-Pz. Div. »H«	477 371 [partly illegible]	23 101 [partly illegible]	29. 9.12 [partly illegible]	T 35 [partly illegible]	30. 1.44 [partly illegible]
4000	Karl Friedrich, I		Kdr. Art. Rgt. 11. SS-Frw. Pz. Gr. Div. »Nl«	1 591 713	101 983	15. 9.11	T 34	1. 3.44
4001	Knöchlein Fritz, I		Kdr. 23. Rgt. 11. SS-Frw. Pz. Gr. Div. »Nl«	157 016	87 881	27. 5.11	B 35	8. 3.44
4002	Eberhardt Erich, I		3. SS-Pz. Div. »T«	*4 178 022*	272 747	19.10.13	B 36	20. 4.44
4003	Braune Fritz, I		Kdr. Pi. Btl. 5. SS-Pz. Div. »W«	416 080	7 916	18. 8.07	T 34	20. 4.44
4004	Kausch Paul, I		Kdr. Pz. Abt. 11. SS-Frw. Pz. Gr. Div. »Nl«	1 736 388	82 578	3. 3.11	B 35	21. 6.44
4005	Barthelmes Helmut		Kdr. Flak. Abt. 8. SS-Kav. Div. »FG«	*2 591 619*	64 457	28. 4.09	B 35	21. 6.44
4006	Geiger Fritz, I II		SS-Führg. H. A.	1 059 405	60 675	7. 2.11	T 34	21. 6.44
4007	von Westernhagen Heinz, I		Kdr. Schw. Pz. Abt. I. SS-Pz. Korps »L«	174 562	41 784	29. 8.11	T 35	21. 6.44
4008	Braun Erich, I		IX. W. Geb. A. Korps-SS	1 210 164	43 733	8. 2.12	T 35	21. 6.44
4009	Radtke Wilhelm, I		4. SS-Pol. Pz. Gr. Div.	—	90 950	22. 5.12	B 36	21. 6.44

Fig 7: *Extract from the SS Dienstaltersliste of November 1944, showing surviving early graduates of the officer schools at Bad Tölz and Braunschweig. Of the 26 Obersturmbannführer mentioned, one (Joachim Peiper) has been awarded the Oakleaves, five the Knight's Cross and 11 the German Cross in Gold. Note also that three officers, including Peiper, were not members of the NSDAP.*

49

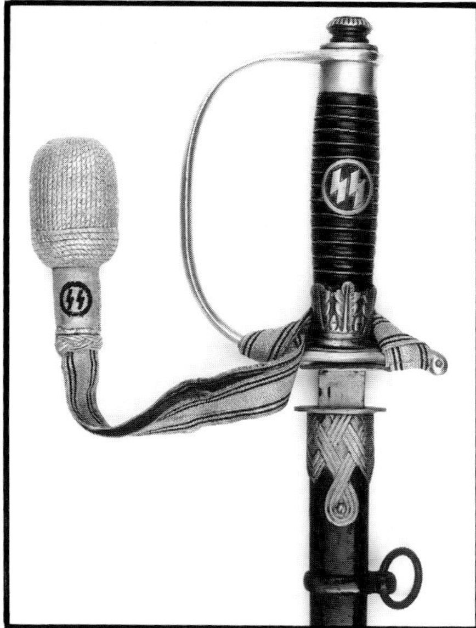

Plate 49: *The Ehrendegen des Reichsführers-SS, or Reichsführer's Sword of Honour, which Himmler bestowed on all graduates of the SS Junkerschulen at Bad Tölz and Braunschweig. Manufacture of the Ehrendegen ceased on 25 January 1941 for the duration of the war, and Waffen-SS officers commissioned after that date frequently reverted to the pre-1936 practice of carrying army sabres. The Ehrendegen has been reproduced since the late 1980s, with many copies featuring the maker's mark of 'F.W. Höller, Solingen' or spurious etched inscriptions on the blade. The SS motto, 'Meine Ehre heisst Treue', never appeared on original swords.*

Plate 50: *Himmler greeting Waffen-SS cavalry officers on the Eastern Front, 24 July 1941.*

Fig 8: *Citation for the German Cross in Gold awarded to Otto Kumm, commander of the 'Der Führer' regiment during the invasion of Russia. It is signed by Field Marshal von Brauchitsch.*

vast majority of non-German officers in the foreign divisions of the SS had their ranks prefixed by 'Legions-' or 'Waffen-' rather than 'SS-' (eg, 'Waffen-Standartenführer des SS') and they, like their men, were not classed as SS members. Because of this, even heroic figures such as Léon Degrelle, holder of the Knight's Cross with Oakleaves and the first recipient of the Close Combat Clasp in Gold, did not merit inclusion in the official SS Officers List.

The summer of 1941 saw the Waffen-SS officer corps in its best condition, and witnessed an influx of recruits from the police, transferred Wehrmacht officers, Party and State officials, doctors, lawyers and youth leaders eager to serve with the new élite. However, the subsequent blood-letting in Russia destroyed the cream of the early graduates of Bad Tölz and Braunschweig and their replacements bore scarcely a token resemblance to them. By 1 July 1943, the officer corps number 10,702. Even so, only 4,145 were designated as career or professional officers, with about 1,000 of them holding ranks of SS-Sturmbannführer and above. Himmler observed at that time that the 'Führerdecke' or 'officer cover' for many frontline SS units was lamentably thin and that the state of the officer corps had deteriorated drastically since the invasion of the Soviet Union.

50

FIG 8

IM NAMEN DES FÜHRERS
UND OBERSTEN BEFEHLSHABERS
DER WEHRMACHT
VERLEIHE ICH
DEM

SS OBERSTURMBANNFÜHRER
OTTO KUMM
KOMMANDEUR SS RGT. „DER FÜHRER"

DAS DEUTSCHE KREUZ
IN GOLD

HAUPTQUARTIER, DEN 3. DEZEMBER 1941

DER OBERBEFEHLSHABER
DES HEERES

51

Plate 51: *Three SS-Hauptsturmführer attached to the 'Handschar' division at the end of 1943. Their decorations indicate that they are German nationals. The officer in the middle, a veteran of the SA/SS rally at Brunswick in 1931, wears the blank right-hand collar patch sported by some 'Handschar' personnel prior to the introduction of the divisional scimitar and swastika patch. Note also the early use of maroon fezzes and Styrian gaiters.* IWM

Three times as many SS officer dossiers survived the war as there were numbers of SS officers in 1941. The great bulk of the remainder related to battlefield commissions granted to Waffen-SS NCOs who had proved themselves at the front between 1942 and 1945. Many thousands of officers were thus added to the corps in a fairly short period of time, men whose ties with the NSDAP and prewar SS were tenuous or even non-existent. The 'military élite' commanding the European SS of 1944 was, therefore, far removed from the politically motivated SS-VT officer corps of the late-1930s. During the last year of the war, Waffen-SS senior officers' conferences saw elderly former Wehrmacht and police officers standing shoulder to shoulder with the younger generation, many of whom had been NCOs or subalterns in 1939 and were now hard-bitten and highly decorated Colonels and Brigadiers. The members of this new officer corps were dubbed by the SS Old Guard as 'Nur-Soldaten' or 'only soldiers', men whose responsibilities were limited to fighting and whose remit did not include the eventual policing of a conquered Europe. The result was a fragmentation of the officer corps between the 'politicals' and the 'fighters', a split which grew ever wider as the war drew to a close. The Waffen-SS uniform never supplanted the Allgemeine-SS membership card in Himmler's mind, and by 1944-45 the typical Waffen-SS officer at the front identified far more with his bloodied Wehrmacht colleagues, and even with his long-suffering enemies, than with his bureaucratic SS seniors in Berlin and Munich.

3 Waffen-SS Uniforms

MANUFACTURE AND SUPPLY

The manufacture of Waffen-SS uniform clothing was undertaken either by private firms, or, increasingly after 1941, by the SS-owned economic enterprises operating under the auspices of the SS Wirtschafts- und Verwaltungshauptamt. The latter were generally set up in concentration camps or prisons and made the maximum use of the cheap labour available.

The first SS clothing factory, or SS-Bekleidungswerke, was established in Dachau concentration camp where the main Waffen-SS clothing depot was also located. In 1939 a training school for tailors and seamstresses opened at Ravensbrück, and after the occupation of Poland and Russia the SS Eastern Industries Ltd, or Ostindustrie GmbH (Osti), used local Jews to manufacture winter uniforms and various items of equipment from property and raw materials seized by the Germans. Civilian clothing confiscated from concentration camp inmates was commonly reprocessed and dyed for transformation into Waffen-SS uniforms.

By 1944, the vast majority of SS and police clothing was being manufactured 'in house' at the following establishments:

- Bayreuth labour camp, Bavaria
- Dachau concentration camp, Bavaria
- Oranienburg concentration camp, near Berlin
- Poniatowa labour camp, near Lublin in Poland
- Posen labour camp, Poland
- Radom labour camp, Poland
- Ravensbrück concentration camp, near Fürstenberg
- Schröttersburg concentration camp, near Plock in Poland
- Straubing prison, Bavaria
- Trawniki labour camp, near Lublin in Poland

Their products sometimes bore the stamp 'SS-BW', followed by a code number allocated to the particular bench or workshop concerned. One of the Dachau codes, for example, was 'SS-BW-0-0453-0058'. Many items manufactured at the SS-Bekleidungswerke were, however, completely unmarked.

The conditions endured by the workers in the camps and prisons were consistently abysmal. Shoddy workmanship automatically resulted in a severe beating, and sometimes death, for the tailor. An 11-hour day was the rule, even during the winter months, with only Sunday afternoons set aside for rest. Food was sparse, debility and mortality increased rapidly, and the productivity of inmates remained far below Himmler's expectations. Almost 500,000 prisoners died during the war from weakness and disease whilst labouring for the SS in their camps and factories.

By 1944-45, shortages of raw materials had created such a crisis in the uniform industry that even the concentration camps could not meet the clothing needs of the Waffen-SS. The result was that newly recruited front-line SS soldiers ended up wearing captured uniforms, particularly Italian items taken after the fall of Mussolini. Older veterans tended to retain their better quality early issue tunics, caps and boots for as long as possible, often until they quite literally fell apart; and there were at least three fully motorised platoons, the so-called SS-Bekleidungs-Instandsetzungszüge 500, 501 and 502, whose sole job it was to travel from unit to unit repairing uniform clothing.

Each Waffen-SS formation regularly submitted requisition forms to the SS Führungshauptamt (SS-FHA) ordering specific uniform needs. If approved, the SS-FHA would instruct the SS Wirtschafts-

und Verwaltungshauptamt (SS-WVHA) to make the necessary issue. The SS-WVHA in its turn then arranged dispatch of the material to the unit, either direct from the factory or via one of its 12 main supply depots, the Hauptwirtschaftslager. Alternatively, the uniform items could be made available to the unit at the nearest convenient SS-WVHA sub-depot, or Truppenwirtschaftslager, of which there were 20 spread out across the Reich. On the Eastern Front, SS supply commands or Nachschubskommandantur were established at Bobruisk, Dnepropetrowsk, Oulu and Riga as links between the SS-WVHA and the local sub-depots. Each supply command was empowered to place contracts with, or make purchases from, private firms in the area. Moreover, where field formations of the Waffen-SS were likely to be operating in a particular area for a prolonged period, for example 'Prinz Eugen' in the Balkans, special *ad hoc* supply bases or Stützpunkte were set up at convenient points.

All Waffen-SS officers were expected to purchase their own uniform items, and newly commissioned officers received a special grant of between 350 and 800 Reichsmarks to that end. Once in possession of his clothing grant the officer was supposed to buy his uniform from one of the SS clothing counters, or Kleiderkasse, at Berlin, Kiev, Lublin, Munich, Oslo, Paris, Prague, Riga and Warsaw. These establishments carried extensive stocks of top quality tailor-made items, including tunics by Mohr & Speyer and Holters, boots by Breitspecher, and caps by Robert Lubstein whose trademark 'EREL' was famous worldwide. However, both the means and opportunity for front-line officers to kit themselves out with expensive uniforms were somewhat limited during the second half of the war, and most relied on their unit stores to provide them with items of field uniform against payment. Standard issue tunics were generally worn unaltered by most officers, although some had them modified to suit individual taste. The most common alterations were to pocket flaps and collars, replacing them with smarter ones. From August 1943, secondhand tailor-made articles began to be collected and re-sold to officers at three times the listed price of their standard issue equivalents. In that way, those who still retained a desire to look 'a cut above the rest' could do so.

On completion of his term of service, every Waffen-SS soldier had to return all issued items of uniform clothing and equipment to his unit. Those still suitable for use were retained intact, and slightly worn items were re-issued to replacement and training units, but old and damaged clothing was sent to the concentration camps to be pulped down for reworking. Damaged metal articles such as belt hooks and buckles were dismantled and sent to the armaments industry for smelting. In that way, the SS maintained a complete cycle of manufacture/issue/wear/pulping/re-manufacture/re-issue in respect of uniform clothing.

52

Plate 52: *Willrich print showing Günther Rauert, a peasant farmer from Todendorf serving as a Sturmmann with the SS-VT Standarte 'Germania' in 1936. He is wearing the black version of the 1934-pattern schiffchen field cap, with death's head button on the front.*

The standard headgear of the Armed SS formations continually evolved from 1933 until the end of World War 2, with every year seeing either a new pattern being introduced, an existing style being modified, or an outdated item being withdrawn.

In March 1933, members of the SS Stabswache 'Berlin' were issued with heavyweight 1916 and 1918 model ex-army steel helmets, hand-painted or sprayed black, for wear when on guard duty. These plain stahlhelme, which did not bear any SS insignia at that time, were the first distinguishing items of headgear to be sported by the armed units. They came in five sizes, and featured distinctive protruding ventilation lugs and either leather or steel liner bands held in place by two-tailed rivets.

During the summer of 1933, field caps identical in cut to those of the Imperial German Army were distributed to men of the SS Sonderkommando Zossen and SS Sonderkommando Jüterbog for wear during training and fatigues. Known as 'Krätzchen' or 'scratchers' because of their rough texture, these black cloth caps were of the peakless 'pork pie' type, circular in cut, with white piping. They bore a metal 1929-pattern eagle and swastika above a Prussian totenkopf, like the insignia seen on Allgemeine-SS headgear. The krätzchen interior featured a waterproof rust-brown fabric with a thin leather sweatband. While the cap was intended strictly for drill use, at least one photograph exists showing it being worn with the black walking-out uniform by two men of the infant Leibstandarte.

At the end of 1933, it was suggested that the 1916 and 1918 model steel helmets were unnecessarily heavy for the Armed SS, whose main role was then one of internal security rather than open warfare. A small number of the army's experimental 1933-pattern vulcanised fibre helmets were duly distributed, but were excessively ugly and proved immediately unpopular. Consequently, during the early part of 1934, the Reichszeugmeisterei der NSDAP or RZM, the Nazi Party's contracts office, placed an order for the supply of new SS helmets which were slightly different in form, weight and appearance from their army counterparts. The RZM-pattern helmet was made of light chromium steel alloy, was marginally less angular in shape, and had the liner band attached by improved solid-core rivets. There were two inspection marks die-stamped inside the neck of the helmet, ie SS runes on the left side and the RZM symbol on the right, and the liner generally bore the unit property stamp in

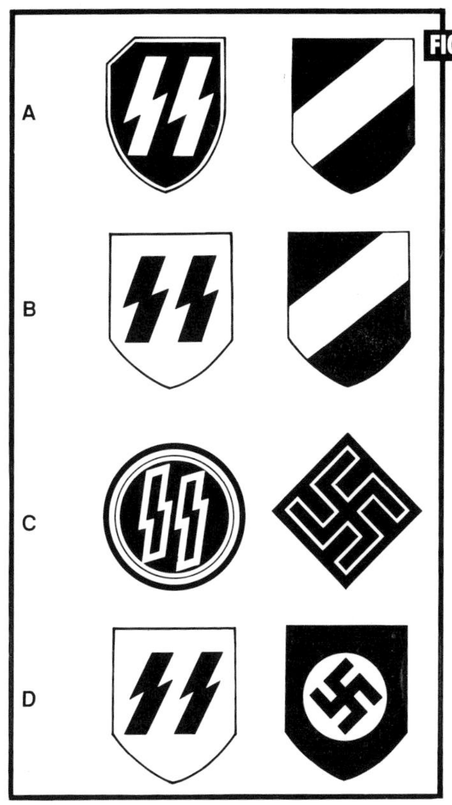

Fig 9: *SS steel helmet insignia. These were worn by soldiers of the following units:*

A Leibstandarte-SS 'Adolf Hitler' (23.2.34-autumn 1934)
B Leibstandarte-SS 'Adolf Hitler' (autumn 1934-11.8.35)
C Politische Bereitschaften and SS-VT formations (23.2.34-11.8.35)
D LAH, SS-VT, SS-TV and all units of the Waffen-SS (12.8.35-1945)

53

Plate 53: *SS-VT personnel on a motor vehicle maintenance course in 1940. The Oberscharführer on the right wears the field-grey peaked cap introduced for NCOs the previous year, while the other SS men sport field-grey M34 schiffchen. The individual third from right, in the black cap, is a civilian mechanic.*

ink, an example being 'II/SS 2'. The RZM helmet was popular, but was suited only for parade and guard duty and was not widely distributed.

On 23 February 1934, special insignia were introduced for wear on all SS steel helmets, hand-painted at first and then in decal form. The Leibstandarte was authorised to use white SS runes on a black shield (soon replaced by black SS runes on a silver shield) on the right side of the helmet, and an army-pattern shield bearing the national colours of black, white and red in diagonal bars on the left side. Troops of the Politische Bereitschaften, and their successors in the SS-VT, wore white-bordered black runes within a white double circle on the right side of the stahlhelm, and a white-bordered black swastika on the left side.

On 15 December 1934, Leibstandarte and SS-Verfügungstruppe steel helmets began to be painted in so-called 'earth-grey', a grey-brown shade, for military manoeuvres. At the same time, a new other ranks' field cap in an identical colour was introduced to replace the black krätzchen. The 1934-pattern cap was again intended for drill use only and was shaped like an upturned boat, hence its nickname 'schiffchen' or 'little ship'. It was made from heavy wool with a cotton lining, and its design was based on the army forage cap first issued about the same time, with a scalloped front and side panels which could be lowered to protect the wearer's ears in cold weather. However, the crease which ran across the top of the SS cap was not centred as in the army style but was set slightly to the right of centre. Moreover, the SS schiffchen also lacked the ventilation holes which were characteristic of the army cap. The first schiffchen were issued with a machine-embroidered version of the 1929-

54

Plate 54: *The other ranks' 1940-pattern schiffchen or 'Feldmütze neuer Art', with machine-woven eagle and death's head.*

pattern eagle on the left side and a plain white metal button to the front. Soon after its introduction, however, the plain button was changed to one featuring an embossed death's head.

In March 1935, troops of the SS-Wachverbände were authorised to wear a large silver-painted Prussian totenkopf on the left side of the steel helmet, to distinguish them from the Leibstandarte and SS-VT. This insignia was short-lived though, for on 12 August 1935 a new set of standardised helmet badges was introduced for all SS units to replace those previously worn. The new insignia, designed by Professor Hans Haas, comprised black SS runes on a silver shield to be worn on the right side of the helmet, and a red shield bearing a white disc containing a black swastika to be worn on the left side. The original order decreed that these badges were to be painted on, but on 14 August it was announced that they would henceforth be available in decal form from the firm of C.A. Pocher of Nürnberg, at a cost of 25 Reichsmarks per 1,000 pairs. They were applied to all SS helmets in time for the NSDAP rally that September.

Towards the end of 1935, an earth-grey version of the black SS peaked cap was introduced for officers of the Leibstandarte and SS-VT, to be worn on all occasions when a steel helmet was not required. The new schirmmütze had an earth-grey woollen or moleskin top with a black velvet band and white piping for all officers up to and including SS-Standartenführer. Higher ranks had silver piping. The peak was made of vulcanised fibre, a lacquered black plastic material, and twisted aluminium chin cords were held in place by two small white pebbled side buttons. Insignia comprised the usual metal eagle and swastika above a death's head. Officers acting as judges and umpires at military exercises wore detachable white cloth bands on their caps. The peaked cap interior generally featured a silk lining and a tan leather sweatband with several rows of perforations towards the front. The underside of the peak was painted a light cream colour.

On 1 November 1936, a supply of the new lighter model army steel helmet, with shallow neck guard, less protruding visor and simple ventilation holes instead of protruding lugs, was set aside by the War Ministry for distribution to the Armed SS. The Leibstandarte and 'Deutschland' received theirs on 11 May 1936, and the other SS-VT formations followed suit. Nevertheless, the old traditional 1916 and 1918 models still continued to be worn for some considerable time particularly by officers.

On 31 March 1935, the other ranks' field cap began to be manufactured in a black version for wear with the black service uniform, and in 'earth-brown' for SS-TV personnel on duty within concentration camps. Insignia remained the same, although the embroidered 1929-pattern eagle was replaced by the distinctive SS type later in the year. The year 1937 saw the general distribution of a new field-grey combat uniform to all branches of the Armed SS, with consequent changes in headgear. The earth-grey and earth-brown schiffchen were replaced by a ubiquitous field-grey version, and the officer's peaked cap also began to be made with a field-grey top.

On 25 February 1938, a new field cap was created for NCOs. It was similar in appearance to the schirmmütze, with a field-grey top, black cloth band and white piping, but the peak was made of the same cloth as the top of the cap and there was no chinstrap or stiffener. It could be folded for storage in a tunic pocket or back-pack, hence its nickname, 'the crusher'. Many NCOs who later became officers continued to wear this popular cap throughout the war, and some individuals hired private tailors to make variants of it with leather peaks, velvet bands and silk linings. The regulation SS badges in white metal were prescribed for the NCO's field cap, but photographic evidence illustrates a wide variety of insignia, both metal and cloth, being worn.

In 1939, a less elaborate version of the field-grey peaked cap was authorised for wear by NCOs in the vicinity of their barracks. It was only after the black uniform had ceased to be worn as walking-out dress that other ranks were issued with, or allowed to purchase, the field-grey peaked cap for walking-out. It was similar to the officer's schirmmütze but had a black leather chinstrap, and a simple cloth band rather than a velvet one.

55

56

Plate 55: *A Waffen-SS NCO wearing the M35 steel helmet on the Eastern Front during the winter of 1941-42.*

Plate 56: *Interior view of an M35 steel helmet, showing the characteristic inward crimping of the rim.*

In June 1939, officers were permitted to purchase a non-regulation white-topped peaked cap for wear with the newly introduced summer uniform. The cap top was made of lightweight white cloth, but otherwise the cap was identical to the standard schirmmütze.

The outbreak of war in September 1939 witnessed the first use by some rear echelon SS units of the so-called Edelstahlhelm, which had previously been issued only to police and fire fighters and was manufactured from a thin gauge steel. Soon afterwards, following army practice, an inverted chevron – or soutache – of braided piping in the appropriate branch of service colour began to be worn on the front of the other ranks' field cap, above the death's head button which was thereafter painted field-grey. Armed SS officers still had no regulation field cap of their own, and during the first few months of the war many of them purchased the 1938 model army officer's forage cap and replaced or covered the national cockade with either a metal SS death's head or a small silver one removed from an army panzer collar patch. This obvious shortcoming in SS headgear was remedied in December 1939, however, when a new field cap was authorised specifically for Waffen-SS officers. It was again boat-shaped but did not have a scalloped front, and the side panels were gently sloping in the style of the Luftwaffe fliegermütze. The top of the flap was piped in aluminium cord and insignia consisted of the SS eagle and totenkopf machine-woven in aluminium wire on a black ground. A waffenfarbe soutache was worn over the death's head. All officers were

Plate 57: *The M42 steel helmet shell was stamped without the edges being crimped inwards, which gave it a sharp appearance around the brim and neckguard.*

57

58

Plate 58: *SS-Gruppenführer Gille was the first Waffen-SS recipient of the Knight's Cross with Oakleaves, Swords and Diamonds. For this presentation photograph, taken on 20 April 1944, he wore a fine example of the General's schirmmütze with aluminium piping.*

instructed to equip themselves with the new field cap by 1 January 1940.

On 21 March 1940, the gaudy black, white and red swastika decal was ordered to be removed from SS steel helmets for the duration of the war, for camouflage reasons. At the same time, helmets began to be painted in a darker shade of field-grey and given a rough surface texture which was less prone to reflecting the light. On 26 March, to simplify the manufacturing process, the old insertable vent bushings were replaced by embossed vents, which became the mark of the 1940-model stahlhelm. In June, an order prohibited further manufacture of the white-topped schirmmütze.

Plate 59: *Interior of a typical officer's peaked cap, showing the celluloid sweat shield, leather sweatband and the silk lining loosely hand-stitched into position.*

59

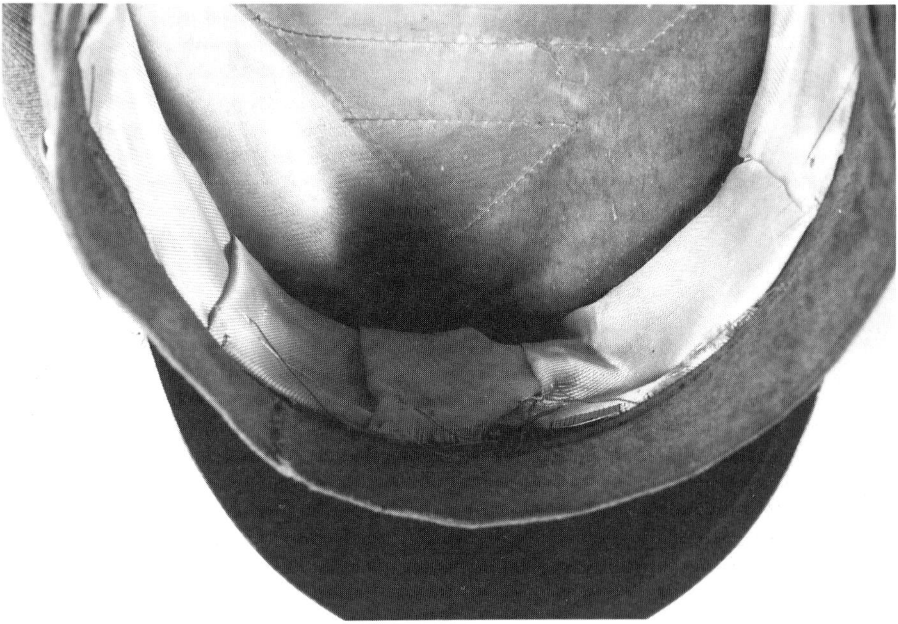

On 15 October 1940, the other ranks' 1934-pattern field cap was replaced by a new style schiffchen identical in cut to the officers' version. It became known as the 'Feldmütze neuer Art' or 'new model field cap', and featured a machine-woven eagle and death's head on the front of the cap instead of the death's head button and side eagle. At first the soutache of waffenfarbe was sewn to the front of the flap, but in order to facilitate the changing of the chevron and cut down on manufacturing time it was soon decided to pass the strip of piping through a loop at its apex and sew it at both ends only.

On 1 December 1940, the fledgling Waffen-SS alpine units received a field-grey Bergmütze or mountain cap to be worn instead of the schiffchen. It was of basic ski-cap design, with a short peak to provide sufficient shade from the glare of the sun and snow. The scalloped side flaps could be lowered to cover the ears, and fastened at the front by means of two small buttons. Officers had aluminium piping around the crown. Insignia comprised a woven death's head on the front of the cap and an eagle on the left side.

In February 1941, the manufacture and retailing of Waffen-SS peaked caps was

60

Plate 60: *The field-grey fez with dark green tassel was issued to members of the Muslim SS divisions 'Handschar' and 'Kama', instead of the Einheitsfeldmütze. Traditionally, Muslim troops wore the peakless fez, and even brimless steel helmets during World War 1 so that they could press their foreheads to the ground during prayer without removing their regulation headgear!*

Plate 61: *'Handschar' troops in festive mood, 1944. The fez has almost completely replaced the schiffchen field cap, and the divisional collar patch is clearly evident.*

61

Plate 62: *On 7 October 1944, Himmler spent his birthday visiting Waffen-SS units on the Western Front. Most of the young SS soldiers in this photograph wear the Einheitsfeldmütze.*

freed from RZM control. From then on the schirmmütze could be made to individual order by private hatters. A variety of makers' labels could subsequently be found inside SS peaked caps, and these were not restricted to German firms. A custom-made 'crusher' cap in the author's collection, for example, which was produced for a Leibstandarte officer stationed in Italy in 1943, bears the trademark 'Successori Fare – Milano/Roma/Toreno/Modena'. As a result of the ever-increasing difficulty in obtaining SS caps and insignia at the front-line, many officers purchased army or police caps, had black bands fitted, and attached the national emblems of the army or NSDAP. Some schirmmützen had the chin cords and stiffeners removed in imitation of the ever-popular 'crusher'.

In March 1941, the 1916, 1918 and RZM-model steel helmets, and any old stocks of earth-grey cloth headgear still in use, were ordered to be withdrawn from service. The following winter saw the first widespread use of fur caps, particularly captured Russian Ushankas, by the Waffen-SS. An almost indescribable range of official, semi-official and unofficial winter caps quickly developed, and the insignia utilised was entirely dependent upon what was available at the time. Metal schirmmütze badges, cloth feldmütze insignia, sleeve eagles and even death's heads cut from SS-Totenkopf-Division collar patches have been observed in photographs.

On 1 August 1942, the smooth inward crimping of the steel helmet rim was abandoned for economic reasons, giving the Model 1942 helmet a sharp silhouette. The next month, the soutache was dropped and no longer featured on field caps.

By 1943, practical experience at the front had shown the schiffchen to be almost useless in comparison to the Bergmütze. On 1 October, therefore, a new field cap was introduced to replace all its predecessors. Known as the Einheitsfeldmütze or standard field cap, it was very similar to the mountain cap but had a longer peak and lower crown. Later versions featured only one fibre or plastic button at the front instead of two metal ones. Insignia was officially a woven death's head to the front and woven eagle to the left side, but schirmmütze badges were frequently used, and the eagle often appeared on the front. Later in the year, a one-piece triangular 'economy' insignia showing both the SS eagle and the totenkopf was authorised, but it was not widely manufactured or distributed. On 1 November 1943, the SS runes helmet decal was discontinued for the duration of the war.

The year 1943 also saw the introduction of the fez, or Tarbusch, for wear instead of the field cap by members of the Muslim SS units. The fez was made from heavy field-grey felt, with a dark green silken tassel and standard woven insignia. The unlined interior had a small thin leather sweatband. A version in maroon was sometimes sported by officers when walking-out or on parade, but may have been unofficial. Albanian Muslims had their own conical fez.

In 1944, Italian SS formations made widespread use of former Italian army field caps, peaked caps and steel helmets, with the addition of appropriate insignia, and in 1945 some Indian volunteers transferred from the Wehrmacht wore turbans with Waffen-SS uniform. For Himmler, that must have been the 'final straw' in the development of SS headgear!

63

Plate 63: *An officer's 'old style' or 'crusher' field cap, which was custom-made in Italy in 1943. It features a leather peak and a narrower than usual black velvet band.*

Plate 64: *The floppy, battle-worn appearance of the 'crusher' cap made it a popular item of headgear right up until the end of the war. Here it is worn by two NCOs of SS-Panzer-Aufklärungs-Abteilung 1 at Kaiserbarracke in the Ardennes, 17 December 1944. The schwimmwagen driver has kitted himself out with a civilian leather motoring helmet.*

64

Members of the first Armed SS units wore the 1932-pattern black service uniform on all occasions. It was identical to the outfit issued to the Allgemeine-SS, but while it was impressive when worn on parade or when walking-out it proved totally impractical for use in the field, or when performing general barrack duties. In order to protect the black uniform in such circumstances, tunics and trousers manufactured from a lightweight grey-white cotton drill were produced in the summer of 1933. Officers and NCOs subsequently wore a drill jacket which was cut very much like the black tunic, although sometimes with concealed buttons, and on which collar patches and a shoulder strap were worn. Other ranks had a less attractive, shapeless, badgeless tunic with a standing collar.

At the beginning of 1935 a new earth-grey uniform, identical in style to the black service outfit, began to be distributed to soldiers of the Leibstandarte and SS-Verfügungstruppe, although it was not referred to in official orders until 25 November of that year. Enlisted men's tunics had five buttons down the front instead of four, and could be worn closed at the neck. Since the standard SS armband with its bright colours was clearly unsuitable for field use, it was replaced on the left arm of the earth-grey tunic by an eagle and swastika. In March 1936, an earth-brown version of the uniform was produced for everyday work-wear by SS-Totenkopfverbände personnel on duty within the confines of concentration camps. It was not to be worn by sentries at the main gate, who were on view to the public, or as a walking-out dress. The earth-brown tunic sported collar patches, a shoulder strap and the SS armband.

In 1937, the earth-grey and earth-brown uniforms of the SS-VT and SS-TV were replaced by a new standardised field-grey uniform. It was based on that of the army, but the feldbluse retained the typically SS features of slanting slash side

Fig 10: *Typical SS combat tunic markings. The maker's SS-BW code number is accompanied by the following regulation size stampings:*
43 length in cm of half-back, ie neck to waist
38 neck size in cm
92 chest size in cm
72 length in cm of full-back, ie neck to hip
62 arm length in cm

FIG 10

SS-BW-0-0453-0058

43 38
92
72 62

pockets and a black and silver-piped collar which was the same colour as the rest of the tunic. The following year, the Leibstandarte began to be issued with army tunics, distinguished by their unpiped dark green collars and pleated patch side pockets, for wear during training.

Plate 65: *A Leibstandarte Obersturmführer is dwarfed by two recruits wearing the lightweight fatigue uniform, autumn 1934. The officer has a tailored grey drill jacket, used in conjunction with the cap and breeches of the black service uniform. Note also the 2nd pattern LAH helmet decals.*

At the end of 1939, the sudden formation of the SS-Totenkopf-Division and the Polizei-Division necessitated their widespread and general use of standard army-issue tunics since there were insufficient quantities of the SS-style field-grey uniform to go round. Because of the basic differences in cut between the two patterns, and Himmler's desire for uniformity of dress, various contradictory orders were issued during the winter of 1939-40, instructing which outfits should be worn by officers as opposed to NCOs and other ranks, when they should be buttoned or unbuttoned at the neck, and so on. These orders were generally ignored by all concerned, and the result was a fair mixture of dress worn simultaneously within even the smallest units.

By May 1940, army tunics had begun to make their inevitable appearance in the ranks of the SS-Verfügungsdivision, and they soon became universal throughout the Waffen-SS. During the course of 1940, their dark green collars were phased out in favour of field-grey ones, and that August the black and silver collar piping was discontinued. From 1942, purely for reasons of economy, patch pockets were made without pleats and in 1943 the lower edges of the pocket flaps were straightened. The wool content of the Model 1943 tunic was

66

Plate 66: *In May 1939, Hitler watched the SS-VT Standarte 'Deutschland' on exercise at the Münsterlager training area. Himmler wears the 1937-pattern field-grey SS tunic with slanting slash side pockets, and a personalised 'crusher' cap which has an army eagle above the death's head. His Old Campaigner's chevron is prominent on the right sleeve.*

also drastically reduced, which resulted in poor thermal insulation and a low tensile strength.

On 25 September 1944, an entirely new style of field service tunic based on the British army battledress blouse was introduced for wear by all German ground combat units, including members of auxiliary formations such as the RAD and NSKK. This uniform required considerably less cloth than the earlier models, and the normal triple or double belt hook location holes were reduced to only one position. Moreover, the internal field dressing pocket was omitted. A universal colour called 'Feldgrau 44', which was more slate grey-green than field-grey, was devised for the new outfit in an effort to standardise the various military and paramilitary uniform colours hitherto seen on the battlefield. However, in reality, many different shades of it emerged. The 1944 field uniform was very unpopular, and was not issued in sufficient quantities to radically change the appearance of the Waffen-SS.

The uniform regulations for Waffen-SS officers differed somewhat from those of other ranks. Until 1939, officers in the Leibstandarte and SS-VT had only one field-grey tunic, the 'Rock' which was identical in cut to the black SS service tunic and was always worn open at the neck with a brown shirt and black tie. At the beginning of the war, some SS officers avoided the expense of having to buy a field blouse for combat wear by having their existing tunics converted, with the addition of stand-and-fall collars which could be closed at the neck. Others had dark green open-necked collars fitted, even though that was expressly forbidden. A number of similar stop-gap measures were taken until the issue of a general order in December 1939, which stipulated that officers' field tunics were henceforth to be identical in style to those of other ranks. Throughout the remainder of the war, Waffen-SS officers generally wore either privately-tailored field blouses like those of their army colleagues, or basic issue tunics purchased from their unit stores. White summer versions were also produced, although these were officially prohibited in June 1940, and the olive green waterproof cotton duck from captured Soviet groundsheets was often made up into lightweight unlined field tunics for hot weather use on the Eastern Front.

As tunics developed, so too did their matching trousers. The 1937-pattern SS field trousers, or Feldhose, had straight legs, two side pockets and a watch pocket in front, and were intended to be worn with jackboots. In July 1942, 'Keilhose' or 'Wedge trousers' were introduced, which had tapered bottoms designed to fit inside

Plate 67: *Soldiers of the Leibstandarte wearing the M36 army pattern tunic with dark green collar and pleated patch side pockets, 19 July 1940.*

68

69

Plate 68: *SS-Sturmbannführer Max Wünsche wearing the officer's open-necked 'Rock' tunic in March 1943.*

Plate 69: *A prewar officer's M37 'Rock' with distinctive slash side pockets, which has been converted for combat wear by the addition of a dark green stand-and-fall collar. Note the other ranks' pattern machine-embroidered runic collar patch, to which officer's piping has been added.* West Point Museum

70

71

Plate 70: *Rolf Möbius, Sepp Dietrich, Rudolf Lehmann and Hubert Meyer in Kharkov, April 1943. Möbius wears a standard issue army pattern field blouse, which is rougher in appearance than the privately-tailored outfits of Dietrich and Lehmann. Meyer's tunic is a converted prewar 'Rock', and still bears the 1936-38 style SS arm eagle.*

Plate 71: *1940-pattern tunic with field-grey collar, as worn by an artillery Rottenführer of the 'Götz von Berlichingen' division, spring 1944. The dress bayonet and knot were carried when walking-out.*

72

73

Plate 72: *A captured SS-Sturmmann of the Leibstandarte is questioned regarding Russian banknotes found in his possession, autumn 1944. He wears the Model 1943 tunic with straight pocket flaps and a late war round-headed arm eagle.* IWM

Plate 73: *Three Waffen-SS medical officers assist personnel of the 15th Scottish Division after the liberation of Neuengamme concentration camp, April 1945. The Untersturmführer on the left wears the 1944 field uniform, which bears a striking resemblance to the British army battledress also shown in the photograph. The man in the centre, with the M42 tunic, has contradictory rank insignia, ie the collar patch of an Untersturmführer and shoulder straps of an Obersturmführer. The Einheitsfeldmütze worn by the third SS officer sports the rarely seen triangular one-piece eagle and death's head insignia.* IWM

the new ankle boots and gaiters. The so-called 'Feldhose 44' were devised as part of the 1944 field uniform, and for the first time featured a built-in cloth waist belt. They had side fob and two hip pockets, one of which was to be used for carrying the field dressing. The bottom of each trouser leg contained a drawstring so that it could be fastened tightly around the ankle. Officers on duty in the field generally wore breeches, with grey buckskin reinforcements on the seat and inside leg. In August 1944, however, they were ordered to wear

74

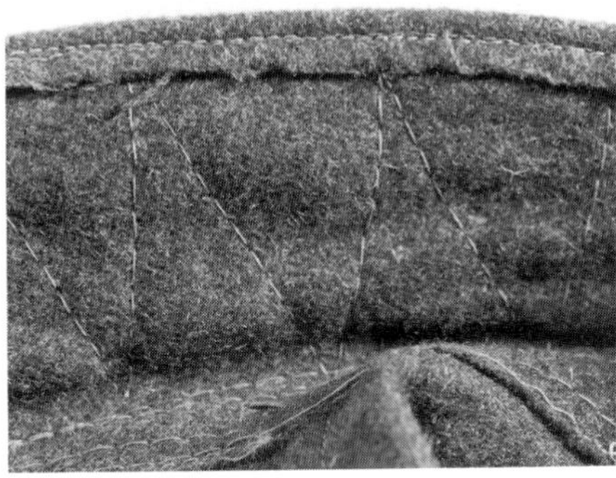

only long trousers, to show a degree of uniformity with their men. Needless to say, that order was seldom adhered to.

While most Waffen-SS units were issued with one or more of the foregoing series of uniforms, depending upon their dates of formation, the Italians alone were not. At the end of 1943, SS-Obergruppenführer Karl Wolff, the HSSPf in Italy, successfully bargained with the army's Quartermaster-General for the supply of 100,000 captured Italian army uniforms for wear by his SS and Police anti-partisan forces. Many of these items were subsequently used to kit out the 24th and 29th SS divisions, whose members duly sported a hodge-podge of Italian garb in grey-green, colonial khaki and mediterranean camouflage, with their own unique insignia.

75

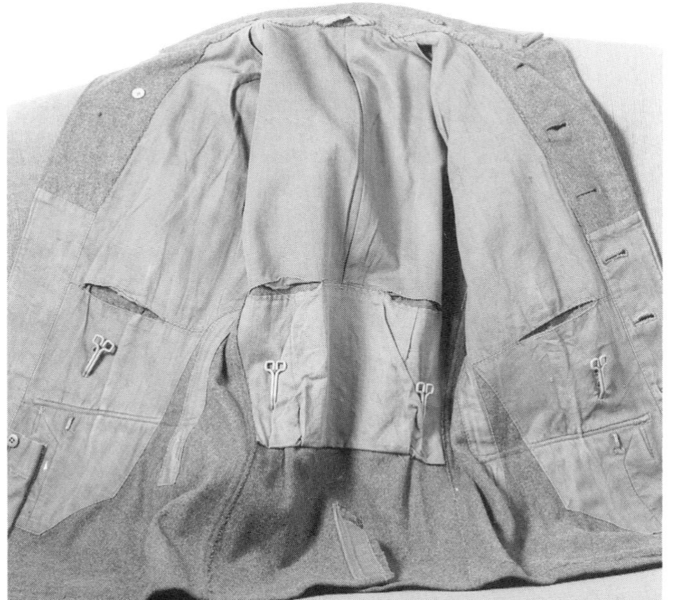

Plate 74: *The distinctive 'zig-zag' pattern of stitching invariably found under the collars of original Waffen-SS tunics.*

Plate 75: *Interior of a typical issue field tunic, showing the partial lining in rough cotton twill.*

The creation of standardised camouflage clothing was the most significant contribution of the Waffen-SS to the history of military uniform development, and had a profound effect on the appearance of all modern soldiery.

In February 1937, SS-Sturmbannführer Wilhelm Brandt, who was a Doctor of Engineering and commander of the SS-VT reconnaissance battalion, began work on the design of camouflage clothing and equipment for use by his troops. He shared his task with the Munich professor Johann Georg Otto Schick, and their prototype camouflage groundsheets and helmet covers were successfully tested by the SS-Standarte 'Deutschland' in field manoeuvres the following December, during which it was estimated that they would reduce battle casualties by 15 per cent. In June 1938, patents in respect of these items were granted to the Reichsführer-SS, so that they could not be copied by the army, and by 1 November contracted production was underway using the firms of Warei, Forster and Joring.

By January 1939, despite great difficulties in obtaining sufficient quantities of waterproof cotton duck and the fact that the fabric had to be printed by hand, 8,400 groundsheets and 6,800 helmet covers had been supplied to the SS-Verfügungstruppe. Smocks were also in course of distribution, and Hausser instructed that at least 20 of these should be held by each company for the exclusive use of assault troops.

Camouflage clothing was not widely worn during the Polish campaign, but even so the revolutionary SS groundsheets and helmet covers earned high praise from Generalmajor Kempf who sent samples of them to the Army High Command in Berlin for evaluation. By June 1940 hand-printing had been superseded by a much faster machine process using 'Anthrasol' and 'Indanthrene' dyes, which allowed the mass production of 33,000 smocks for delivery to all field units of the Waffen-SS. The ever present problem however, even at that early date, was the shortage of raw materials. It was calculated that over 42,000 metres of waterproof cotton duck would be required every month to produce sufficient numbers of groundsheets, helmet covers and smocks, and by January 1943 supplies had all but completely run out, resulting in its replacement by drill material which had no waterproof qualities.

Many variant styles of camouflage were ultimately manufactured simultaneously, including the so-called 'oak-leaf', 'plane tree', 'burred edge', 'palm tree',

76

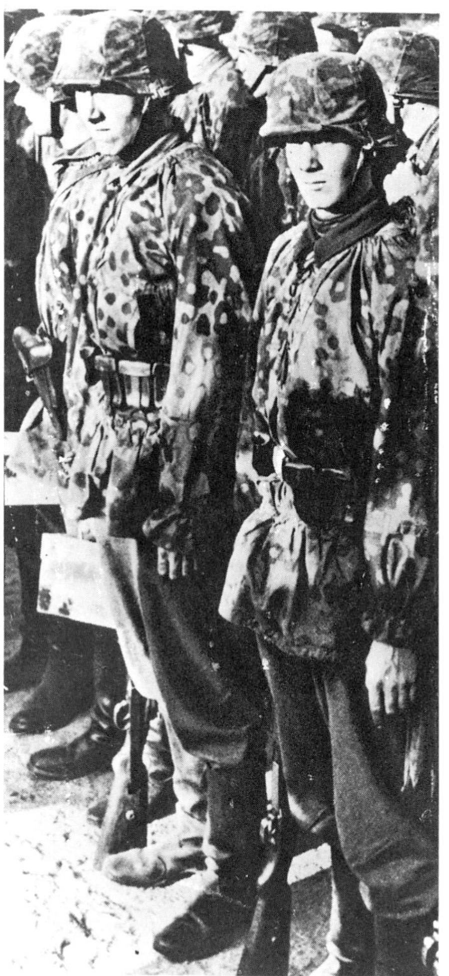

Plate 76: *SS assault troops wearing newly issued camouflage smocks and helmet covers, May 1940.*

'flower' and 'clump' patterns. Four colours were generally used, and the tendency during the war was towards increasingly spotted designs in lighter shades. Most garments made from waterproof cotton duck were printed on both sides and were reversible, with one side predominantly green and the other brown for use as local and seasonal variations dictated. The later drill outfits were printed on one side only and could not be reversed. All of these patterns were issued indiscriminately throughout the Waffen-SS.

Fig 11: *Early pattern Waffen-SS camouflage smock,.with vertical openings at the front, absence of foliage loops, and no pockets in the skirt. Note in particular the construction of the sleeves.*

The groundsheet or Zeltbahn was the first item of camouflage uniform to see widespread distribution amongst SS units.

77

Plate 77: *SS-Obersturmführer Gerhard Bremer, who won the Knight's Cross on 30 October 1941 as commander of the Leibstandarte's 1st Motorcycle Company. He wears the early pattern helmet cover, without foliage loops.*

It was triangular in shape, measuring 203cm x 203cm x 240cm, and could be worn as a cape or poncho, or buttoned together with three others to form a four-man tent. In fact, any number could be combined to make even larger shelters. When attaching Zeltbahnen in such circumstances care had to be taken to use identical, or at least similar, pattern groundsheets to maintain the camouflage effect, and to that end identifying pattern numbers were printed along their bases. Even when combining shelter quarters of different designs, 'paving slabs' of colour were provided along the edges at regular intervals so that the various camouflage patterns would merge into each other. In December 1943 it was decided not to issue any more groundsheets to men on the Eastern Front for economy reasons, and by September 1944 their production had ceased completely

The steel helmet cover was produced from segments of Zeltbahn material, and consequently occasionally featured the identifying printed pattern number. It was designed to conform to the shape of the Model 1935 stahlhelm and was attached by means of three spring-loaded blackened steel clips held on by bare aluminium rivets, one at each side and one at the rear. The 1937 prototype also had a fourth frontal clip, but that was later replaced by a simple fold of material and was never subsequently adopted for field use. Covers made from 1942 onwards had loops sewn on to hold foliage.

The camouflage smock was a reversible pullover garment gathered at the neck by means of an adjustable cord and at the wrists and waist by elastic. It had no collar and the first pattern had no pockets, only two vertical openings at the front which gave the wearer access to his tunic underneath. During the war, various modi-

78

Plate 78: *An SS-Sturmmann with the M42 camouflage field cap.*

fications were made to it including the adoption of a longer 'skirt', foliage loops sewn in threes to the shoulders and upper sleeves, and the addition of two side pockets with buttoned flaps. However, all smocks conformed to the standard manufacturing process of being cut out from a long strip of Zeltbahn material, with a central hole for fitting over the head. They were sewn only up the sides, never across the shoulders, and the sleeves were always made up from two or three segments stitched together. Production ceased in January 1944, although smocks continued to be widely worn until the end of the war.

On 15 April 1942 a camouflage face mask, which had initially been rejected by Hausser during prewar trials, was issued for use in conjunction with the helmet cover and smock. It comprised a series of strings fitted to an elasticated strap and hung like a curtain over the face. The mask was very effective when used in bushy terrain and was much prized by snipers.

On 1 June 1942 a camouflage field cap, again made from waterproof Zeltbahn material, was introduced. It was shaped like the Bergmütze and was generally unlined and reversible. From December that year, special insignia woven in green and brown artificial silk were produced for wear on the cap, but they do not appear to have been widely adopted.

On 1 March 1944, a camouflage version of the drill uniform was introduced for both field and working dress. It comprised a tunic and trousers in the same cut as the Model 1943 field uniform, but made from lightweight unlined herringbone twill with a standardised spotted or 'pea' pattern camouflage printed on one side only. It could be worn on its own during the summer, or on top of a standard field uniform in cold weather, and was designed to replace the smock and, ultimately, the normal field and drill uniforms. Only the eagle and swastika and special rank badges were intended to be worn on the left sleeve of the tunic, but shoulder straps and other insignia were also occasionally seen. Between 1 November 1944 and 15 March

Plate 79: *An assault squad of the 'Nord' division in the Karelian forests east of Kiestinki, Finland, February 1944. Several of the soldiers have hung anti-mosquito nets over their steel helmets.*

Plate 80: *The Model 1944 'pea' pattern camouflage drill tunic as worn by a Waffen-SS infantry Obersturmführer, 1944-45. The unofficial display of insignia and decorations, the use of an Iron Cross 2nd Class as a 'Feldritterkreuz' or 'Frontline Knight's Cross', and the preference for the sturdy other ranks' belt buckle typified the appearance of junior SS officers towards the end of the war.*

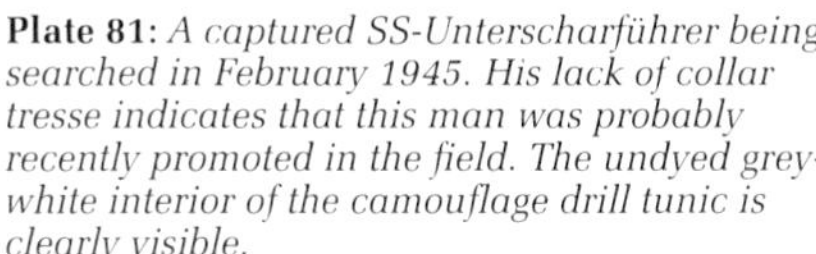

Plate 81: *A captured SS-Unterscharführer being searched in February 1945. His lack of collar tresse indicates that this man was probably recently promoted in the field. The undyed grey-white interior of the camouflage drill tunic is clearly visible.*

Plate 82: *Inside view of the camouflage drill tunic, showing belt hook supports and lack of lining.*

81

82

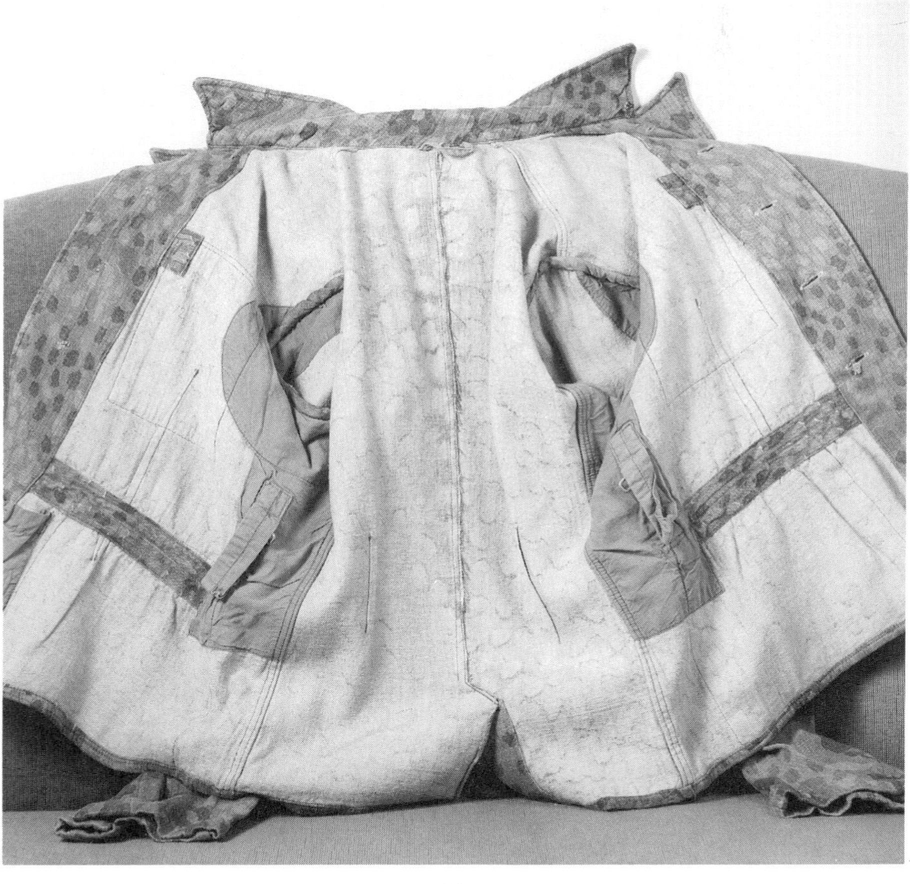

83

1945, distribution of the camouflage drill uniform was suspended because of its intolerable losses during the winter months. In effect, it was never reissued.

While the vast majority of Waffen-SS troops wore one or more of the foregoing camouflage garments, there were many instances of non-regulation items being adopted. It was not unknown for tunics to be tailor-made in the field from spare Zeltbahn material, and large quantities of caps, tunics and trousers in German cut were manufactured from captured Italian camouflage material in 1944. There were also isolated cases of Waffen-SS personnel, particularly members of the 14th Division, wearing German army-pattern camouflage smocks. A photograph even exists apparently showing the capture of an SS sniper in Normandy who is wearing the one-piece camouflage coverall issued to US troops serving in the Pacific theatre. However, that may well have been a 'propaganda' shot staged by the Allies.

Plate 83: *During their first week of action in Normandy, these three soldiers of the 'Hitlerjugend' division won the Iron Cross. The man on the left wears a regulation smock and has pinned a metal death's head to his M42 camouflage field cap. The others have been kitted out with jackets in Italian camouflage material. Note also the use of civilian scarves.*

By 1945 it had become apparent that both the Wehrmacht and Waffen-SS should ideally have one common camouflage pattern. After various tests and trials carried out by Schick and three SS officers from the Bekleidungswerke at Dachau, a new design, incorporating carbon black segments which had the effect of protecting the wearer against infra-red detection, was introduced under the name 'Leibesmuster'. It never saw distribution during the Third Reich, but was later adopted by the Bundeswehr and is still worn to this day by the Swiss army.

The tank troops of most European armies of the 1930s were issued with protective, tight-fitting black uniforms for wear when working on, or operating in, their vehicles. These were generally designed as practical outfits for men who had to serve in the confined spaces of a tank, crammed with potentially dangerous pieces of metal and covered with oil and dirt. The German army's version was introduced in November 1934 and was soon regarded as an 'élite uniform', which led to its being worn on every possible occasion, not only by crew members but also by other ancillary personnel serving with panzer regiments.

SS-VT armoured troops received their own black panzer uniform in 1938. Its special headgear took the form of a floppy black woollen beret, or Baskenmütze, fitted over an internal crash helmet, the Schutzmütze, which comprised a heavily padded liner. A large embroidered SS eagle and a uniquely designed totenkopf, not unlike the army's panzer death's head but with a lower jaw in the SS style, were sewn on to the front of the beret. The Baskenmütze was discontinued in 1940 after proving impractical in combat. It was replaced by a black version of the schiffchen field cap, which was in turn superseded by a black Einheitsfeldmütze in October 1943.

The SS tank tunic, or Panzerjacke, was a short double-breasted black jacket fastened with concealed buttons. It differed from its army counterpart in that the front was cut vertically instead of being slanted, the lapels were smaller and there was no central seam down the back. The collar of the jacket was piped in silver for officers but was unpiped for other ranks, and only NCOs of the Leibstandarte were permitted to sport their regulation collar tresse. The trousers accompanying the Panzerjacke were baggy and had the bottoms fastened around the ankles by drawstrings and footstraps.

Plate 84: *On 9 July 1940, the reconnaissance battalion of the SS-Verfügungsdivision crossed the Hendaye Bridge on the Franco-Spanish border to form a guard of honour at a meeting between Hitler and General Franco. These men are from the armoured car platoon and wear the SS panzerjacke and the ill-fated Baskenmütze, which was discontinued shortly thereafter.*

84

85

86

Plate 85: *The PzKpfw III command tank of 1st battalion, 3rd SS-Panzer-Regiment, 'Totenkopf' division, in southern Russia during November 1943. The officer on the left is SS-Hauptsturmführer Erwin Meierdrees, holder of the Knight's Cross with Oakleaves, who was killed in action near Dunaalmas, Hungary, 4 January 1945.*

Plate 86: *SS-Untersturmführer Michael Wittmann and his Leibstandarte Tiger crew after being decorated in January 1944. They were killed near Caen seven months later, but not before they had become the most successful team of tank soldiers in history, destroying over 270 enemy vehicles.*

In the spring of 1941, a field-grey version of the panzer uniform was issued to members of the Leibstandarte's Sturmgeschütz-Abteilung. By August 1942 this outfit had been distributed to other assault gun units, and four months later its wear was extended to all Waffen-SS anti-tank formations. At least one field-grey example of the SS panzer beret exists, and is said to have been used exclusively by crews of Opel Maultier self-propelled rocket launchers during 1943. However, given that the early black berets were decreed useless and withdrawn from service in 1940, ie before the introduction of the field-grey panzer uniform, and that their crash liners were re-used in the manufacture of winter fur hats, this explanation seems extremely dubious. No photographs showing a field-grey SS beret in wear have yet come to light, and it is very possible that the existing piece is a postwar creation.

In September 1941, a lightweight panzer uniform in reed-green denim drill material was distributed to crews of tanks and armoured cars to be worn as a work or summer outfit. It was instantly popular and remained so throughout the war. Although the basic cut of the reed-green uniform remained unchanged, there were minor modifications at various stages, foremost amongst which was the addition of large patch pockets with flaps to the left front of the jacket and left thigh of the trousers.

On 15 January 1943, panzer crews received a one-piece combination work uniform made of camouflage waterproof cotton duck, identical to the material used in the manufacture of the smock and Zeltbahn. These coveralls were usually worn without insignia, although shoulder straps were occasionally sported. At the same time a winter combination was introduced, made from two thicknesses of cloth, white on one side and field-grey on the other, and was widely worn during the Battle of Kharkov.

These coverall combination outfits were never very popular, simply because of the difficulty of getting in and out of them. That fact, allied with the success of the reed-green denims and the extreme shortage of waterproof cotton duck, led to the decision being made in January 1944 to discontinue the camouflage combination and produce instead a lightweight version of the panzer uniform in camouflage herringbone twill. It duly appeared two months later, at the same time as the camouflage drill uniform introduced for all other Waffen-SS units, and it was in the same standardised spotted 'pea' pattern, unlined and printed on one side only. The camouflage panzer uniform saw widespread service, particularly on the Western Front. On 1 November distribution ceased for the duration of the winter, and the camouflage outfit was never reissued.

While the clothing of Waffen-SS armoured personnel remained fairly standard, there was one major initiative at divisional level which drastically altered the appearance of many panzer crews participating in the Normandy campaign. During the autumn of 1943, the Leibstandarte had been involved in disarming capitulated Italian armed forces and fighting partisans in northern Italy. In the process, the division had confiscated huge quantities of abandoned Italian motor transport and uniform equipment to supplement its own limited supplies. Amongst the uniform items seized were large numbers of German U-boat leather jackets and trousers, originally sold by Hitler to Mussolini's navy, and vast stocks of Italian army camouflage material. The latter was quickly used to produce caps, tunics and overalls in the German style, which were distributed to soldiers of the Leibstandarte and 'Hitlerjugend' in France. The U-boat clothing went almost exclusively to the young tank crews of 'Hitlerjugend', and duly protected many of them against serious burns.

SS-Fallschirmjäger-Bataillon 500 was formed for 'special duties' at the end of 1943, in the wake of SS-Hauptsturmführer Otto Skorzeny's much-vaunted liberation of the deposed Mussolini that September, which had needed to rely on Luftwaffe glider and paratroop support. Contrary to widespread belief, the battalion was not a penal unit. It was composed entirely of volunteers, fully trained in a paratroop role, and all its officers and NCOs were professional soldiers with a great deal of frontline experience. This expertise, combined with the Waffen-SS ethos, produced paratroopers of outstanding ability.

The first major action in which the battalion was deployed, Operation 'Rösselsprung' or 'Knight's Move', involved its being dropped by glider right on top of Marshal Tito's vast partisan headquarters complex at Bastasi, near Drvar in Yugoslavia, where Winston Churchill's son, Major Randolph Churchill, was head of the British military mission. The plan was to capture Tito on his birthday, 25 May 1944, and hold him until support could arrive from the 'Prinz Eugen' division and other nearby conventional ground formations. However, the SS paras were too small a force to take on the partisan brigade entrenched in the mountain fortress, and they were surrounded in Drvar cemetery and almost wiped out. The survivors were reformed as SS-Fallschirmjäger-Bataillon 600, under Skorzeny's command, and trained for a drop on Budapest to capture the son of the recalcitrant Hungarian leader Admiral Horthy. The latter gave in to other German units without a fight. Some SS paratroops were later involved in the Ardennes offensive and the remainder fought as infantry on the Eastern Front, going into captivity at the end of the war.

Of all the branches of the Waffen-SS, least is known about the clothing and equipment of the parachutists. No official uniform orders have come to light, and almost total reliance has to be placed on a few extant wartime photographs. It appears that the Luftwaffe assumed responsibility not only for the training and transportation by air of the SS paras, but also for supplying them with specialist dress and equipment. When Skorzeny and his small joint SS and Luftwaffe commando force rescued Mussolini from his imprisonment at Gran Sasso, they all wore regulation air force tropical clothing with full Luftwaffe insignia. At a celebratory rally held in the Berlin Sports Palace soon afterwards, however, the SS men reverted to their normal field-grey uniforms.

The members of SS-Fallschirmjäger-Bataillone 500 and 600 wore 1940-pattern SS schiffchen field caps, SS belt buckles and standard Waffen-SS field-grey tunics with the insignia of their previous units, since there were no specialist SS paratroop badges. The Luftwaffe supplied all their protective clothing, which comprised: the normal paratroop steel helmet, with or without the air force eagle decal and geometric 'splinter' pattern camouflage cover/string netting; the 'splinter' pattern camouflage paratroop smock, with or without Luftwaffe breast eagle; blue-grey or field-grey paratroop trousers; canvas gaiters; and ankle boots. One surviving photograph shows two German paratroopers wearing standard SS-issue camouflage smocks, but these are thought to be Luftwaffe Fallschirmjäger personnel in Italy, who would have had the opportunity of obtaining SS smocks from the 'Hermann Göring' panzer division, which was kitted out with them. Another unique picture illustrates an SS paratrooper apparently wearing the 'pea' pattern camouflage drill tunic and trousers while fulfilling an infantry role on the Eastern Front near the end of the war.

During recent years, several references have been made to a batch of paratroop smocks manufactured from SS 'pea' pattern camouflage drill material with the SS eagle stitched to the right breast. These appeared in the USA during the early 1980s with the story that they had been found by American troops occupying the SS-Bekleidungslager at Dachau in April 1945. It was alleged that the smocks had thereafter been taken back to the US as a 'job lot', for wear by sportsmen when duck shooting! While such tales cannot be disproved, there must be great doubt as to the authenticity of these items. For one thing, markings

stamped inside some of the smocks give the date '1943', plausible so far as the formation of the SS parachute battalion is concerned but a year early for the 'pea' pattern camouflage! If made in 1943, why were they not worn at Drvar and, indeed, never issued at all? Every example viewed has been in absolutely 'new' condition, showing no signs of age whatsoever. Moreover, no wartime references to, or photographs of, the SS paratroop smock exist. Some stocks of 'pea'pattern camouflage drill material survived the war, and it is now being reproduced for the 'battle re-enactment' fraternity, so the postwar creation of 'SS para smocks' would not have been difficult, a point reinforced by the sudden appearance of a pair of never-before-heard-of 'pea' pattern paratroop trousers in France in 1990. The situation has not been helped by the fact that several major museums, including the Bastogne Museum, have purchased examples of these smocks assuming them to be genuine and have displayed them amongst original militaria. In the end analysis, all of these so-called 'ex-Dachau' items must be considered with the deepest suspicion.

Plate 87: *SS paratroopers entrenched in the defensive positions around Schwedt on the Eastern Front, February 1945. All wear Fallschirmjäger helmets, and the men in the foreground have standard Waffen-SS field-grey tunics.*

An 'SS-Fallschirmjäger' cuff title exists in various styles, both embroidered and woven. It is a postwar fantasy piece, first produced in the 1970s. No SS paratroop cuff title existed during the Third Reich, and the few cuff titles worn by SS paras were those of their former units.

While Waffen-SS troops never served in North Africa, a few units, primarily the Leibstandarte, 'Wiking', 'Prinz Eugen' and 'Reichsführer-SS', saw action in the Balkans, southern Russia and Italy, where the sweltering summer conditions made the wearing of conventional uniform items very uncomfortable indeed. However, the demand for hot weather clothing was usually localised and temporary, so the development of a tropical uniform for the Waffen-SS was gradual and on something of an *ad hoc* basis.

The first requirement for tropical clothing was voiced in April 1941, during the hastily organised invasion of Greece, but on 15 April Himmler specifically prohibited his officers from using the recently introduced army tropical outfit. Consequently, troops of the Leibstandarte completed their race through the country wearing heavy regulation tunics and headgear which proved far from ideal. Some members took to wearing the basic SS sports kit, comprising vest and shorts, when not engaged in combat while others went bare-chested. A short-term partial solution was achieved by the issue of German, Italian, Dutch and captured British pith helmets or Tropenhelme, diverted from the army's 5th Light Division. However, these items were generally unpopular and were not worn in any great numbers. When sported by the SS, they bore no insignia. A number of

Plate 88: *The Waffen-SS garrison in Milan lays down its arms, 30 April 1945. The soldiers on the left wear the regulation SS tropical field cap.*

88

original Tropenhelme survive featuring metal SS runic and swastika shield badges in the same style as the standard SS steel helmet decals. Even so, there is no evidence to support the notion that SS Tropenhelme insignia existed prior to 1945. Indeed, the swastika shield decal had been discontinued on 21 March 1940, a year before the introduction of sun helmets to the SS! It is likely that these metal SS shields are postwar creations.

During the autumn of 1942, SS-Division 'Wiking' advanced deep into the Caucasus region and the real need for hot weather clothing again became apparent. Following upon Himmler's prohibition on the wear of the army's olive-green tropical uniform, a small number of 'Wiking' personnel adopted the Luftwaffe's version instead. It was made from light tan cotton drill and comprised an unlined four-pocket tunic, schiffchen field cap and baggy trousers. All Luftwaffe insignia were removed and replaced by standard SS badges from the field-grey uniform. On 15 February 1943, SS chevrons in tan-brown on black were created for wear with the tropical tunic by personnel of the ranks of Sturmmann and Rottenführer. At the same time, the use of collar patches with the tropical tunic was forbidden.

In September 1943 a wholly new and, for the first time, formalised Waffen-SS tropical uniform was introduced and distributed on an entire unit basis to the Sturmbrigade 'Reichsführer-SS' on Corsica. The uniform tunic was a strange hybrid, having pleated patch pockets in the army style, being coloured light tan in the Luftwaffe style, and featuring a caped effect across the upper section in the Italian Sahariana style, the peaks of the 'cape' forming the upper pocket flaps. All buttons were removable, being attached by split rings. Insignia was officially restricted to shoulder straps, tropical sleeve chevrons and a special tan-brown woven version of the SS arm eagle, but normal collar patches were also occasionally seen. Markings on an example of this tunic previously in the author's collection suggests that it was manufactured in the SS-Bekleidungswerke at Straubing.

The SS tropical field cap, to accompany the new tunic, was in the same shape as the Einheitsfeldmütze, but without the flap and buttons. Cut like the SS camouflage field cap, it was again light tan in colour and sported a tan-brown woven eagle and death's head. No officer's version existed. The outfit was finished off with a tropical shirt, trousers, shorts and boots, supplied from Luftwaffe stocks.

Photographic evidence suggests that the 1943-pattern Waffen-SS tropical tunic was only ever issued to the Sturmbrigade 'Reichsführer-SS', and even then was not worn by members of that formation after they left Corsica to become the nucleus of the 16th SS-Panzergrenadier Division. The Sturmbrigade, a force of around 2,000 men which grew from Himmler's escort battalion, appears to have been chosen to field-test and evaluate the new tunic on an experimental basis. Whether it was badly reported upon, or whether economies and the lack of tropical campaigns after 1943 dictated that no more stocks of the tunic would be manufactured, is unknown. In any event, there is nothing to indicate that it was issued again. The SS tropical field cap, on the other hand was widely distributed amongst various units fighting in Italy during 1944-45, and was a popular item of dress.

During the last year of the war, members of SS units fighting in Italy, Austria and the Balkans reverted to wearing a mixture of Wehrmacht and Italian tropical clothing, as and when availability and climate dictated. Luftwaffe items were most prized, particularly the tunic and schiffchen, and the latter could often be seen sporting SS metal badges removed from the peaked cap. Moreover, despite the versatility of the camouflage helmet cover, it was not unknown for Waffen-SS men to paint their steel helmets sand-yellow while serving in the Mediterranean area.

Various items of protective clothing were widely distributed to Waffen-SS personnel, irrespective of their branch of service.

As early as July 1935, the Leibstandarte was issued with an earth-grey double-breasted greatcoat, or Mantel, which bore collar piping and full insignia. This item was superseded by a field-grey version in 1937, and with the military development of the SS-VT and SS-TV there was a tendency to closely follow army greatcoat fashions, which led to the gradual adoption of a dark green collar and the *ad hoc* removal of collar patches. By the outbreak of war, the situation as regards greatcoat insignia was fairly muddled and various orders were issued in an attempt to clarify the position. The dark green collar was officially approved in December 1939, only to be cancelled a few months later. Collar piping for other ranks became obsolete in August 1940, and all surviving examples of the old earth-grey coat were recalled in March 1941. Officers with the rank of SS-Oberführer and above were privileged in being allowed to wear the greatcoat with the top three buttons undone, so as to expose their distinctive silver-grey lapels, and from 1941 holders of the Knight's Cross or any other neck award were also permitted to do so, for the purpose of displaying their decorations. As the war progressed, many officers countered the declining quality of the issue Mantel by having greatcoats tailor-made to their own specifications. These items incorporated such refinements as removable blanket linings, reinforced buttons, extra internal pockets and detachable sheepskin or fur collars. The result of all this was that dozens of variations on the basic Waffen-SS greatcoat came to be produced and worn side by side, many of them in contravention of regulations. Moreover, a massive version of the Mantel, called the

Plate 89: *Tailor-made winter greatcoat, with heavy fur lining, worn by Sepp Dietrich on the Eastern Front. Note the silver-grey lapels of an SS General.* West Point Museum

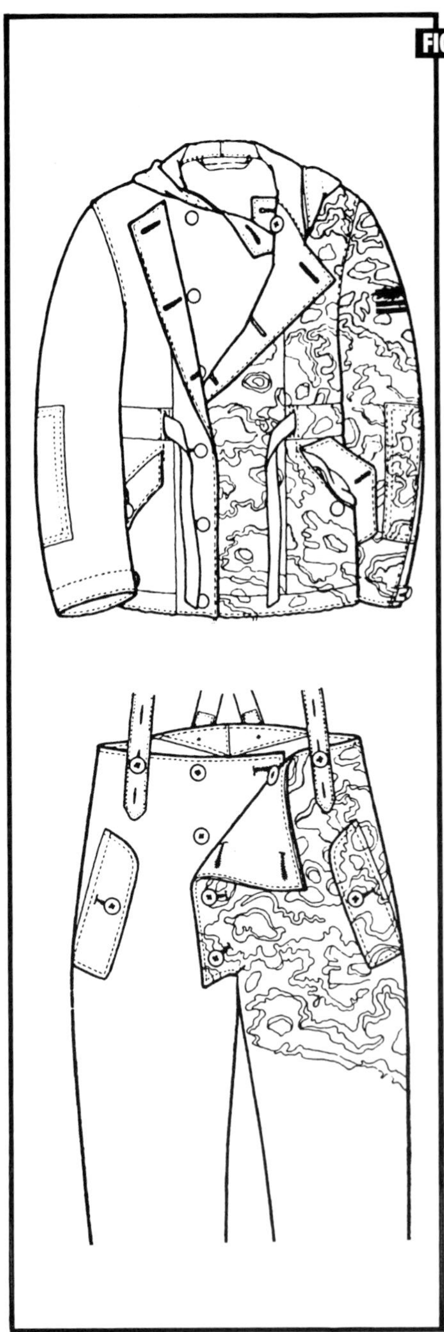

Fig 12: *The 1943-pattern SS winter uniform, comprising reversible jacket and trousers.*

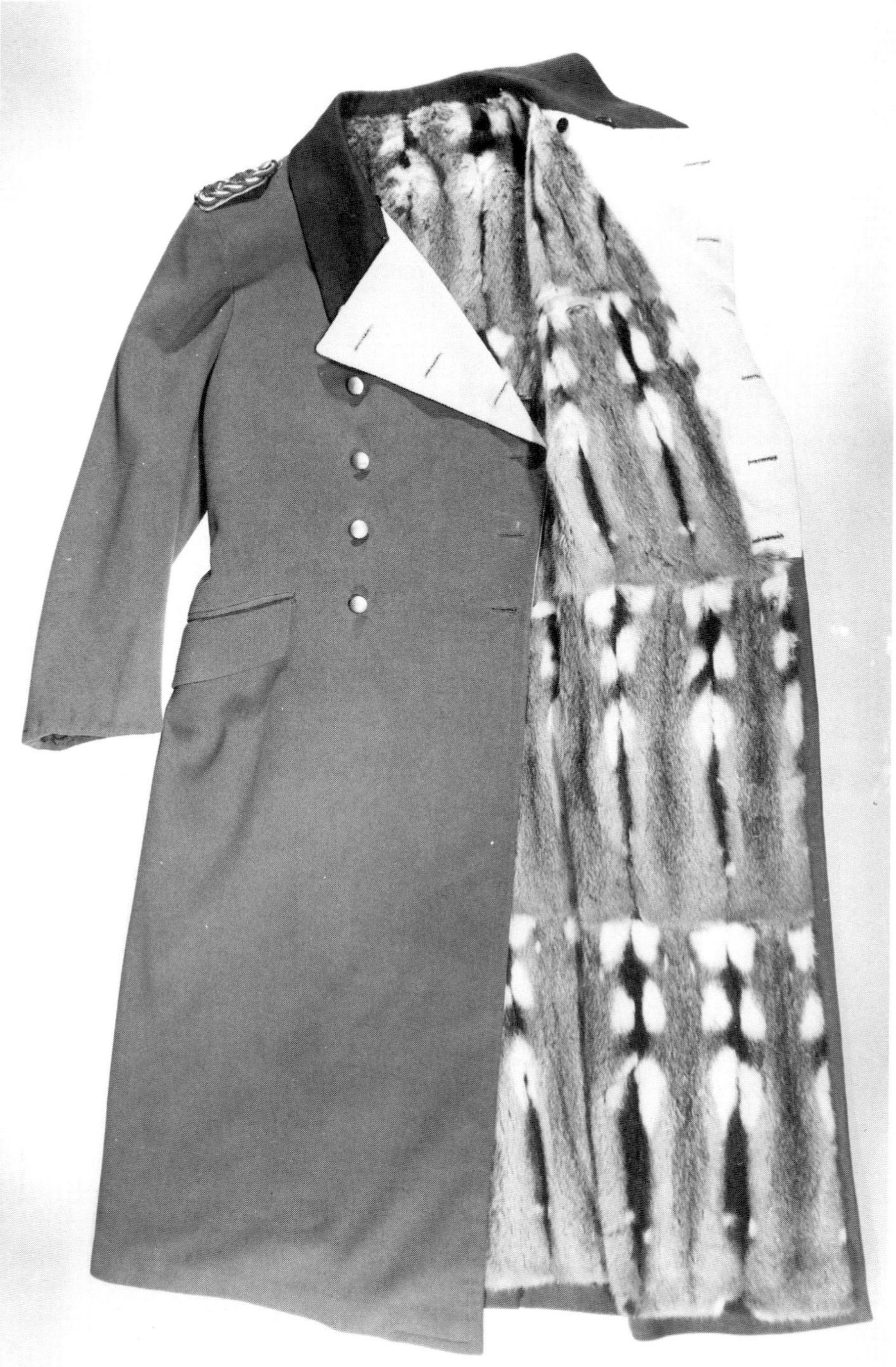

90

Plate 90: *Sepp Dietrich's field-grey leather greatcoat, with SS-Obergruppenführer shoulder straps. It bears the maker's label of 'Schuchart & Tschach, Dresden'.* West Point Museum

Plate 91: *SS troops wearing the standard issue greatcoat in Kharkov, 15 March 1943.*

91

surcoat or Übermantel, was designed to be worn on top of the ordinary greatcoat by drivers of open motor vehicles or those on static sentry duty, and featured two vertical pockets above the waist in addition to the normal side pockets.

Officers had the option of purchasing a field-grey leather greatcoat, but this item was extremely expensive and few subalterns could afford it. There were several variants, both in cut and in the use of insignia. As an alternative to the Ledermantel, many junior officers and NCOs bought the much cheaper 1938-pattern field-grey raincoat, the so-called Regenmantel, made of rubberised cotton twill with a leather-like appearance. Others used the regulation motorcyclist's coat, or Kradschutzmantel, which was first introduced for army dispatch riders and eventually came to be widely worn by a variety of Wehrmacht, Waffen-SS and Police personnel during inclement weather. Early examples had a dark green cloth collar, but after 1940 the whole coat was made from rubberised fabric. The skirt could be divided and buttoned around the legs for ease of use on the motorcycle.

Following the disastrous winter campaign of 1941-42, when no adequate warm clothing was provided for German soldiers fighting on the Russian Front, preparations were made to design and supply appropriate uniform items with a view to averting a similar crisis. Various fur, sheepskin and lambswool waistcoats were issued in the short term, and snow anoraks originally intended for mountain troops serving in Norway were diverted and shipped east. Wherever shortages were still apparent, captured Soviet winter clothing was issued, augmented by civilian items collected in Germany.

92

Plate 92: *'Totenkopf' troops in Kharkov, March 1943. The tank commander, whose cap death's head has almost fallen off, sports an unofficial sheepskin waistcoat, while his colleague has been issued with the fur-lined cement-grey parka.*

93

Plate 93: *Even the fur-lined winter combat uniform could not always provide sufficient warmth. This miserable-looking Waffen-SS machine-gunner on a static position in the Toropez forest at the end of 1943 has had to resort to wrapping a blanket around his legs and feet.*

94

Throughout 1942, the Waffen-SS developed its own winter combat uniform, or Winter-Sonderbekleidung, independent of the army. It consisted of a heavy fur-lined parka-type coat in a waterproof cement-grey gabardine, with matching overtrousers. When snow lay on the ground, an undyed white cotton hooded smock and trousers were issued. These were designed to be worn on top of the parka and overtrousers, and were readily washable. At the end of the year a padded reversible parka in a waterproof rayon, white on one side and tan or reed-green on the other, was distributed for use as a windcheater.

The definitive Waffen-SS winter uniform did not enter service until 1943-44 and comprised a hood, jacket, trousers and mittens all made from two layers of windproof material with a wool-rayon interlining. The whole outfit was reversible, being white on one side and SS autumn camouflage on the other, and was designed to be worn over the normal field uniform. The white side tended to get filthy very quickly, which defeated its purpose, so troops were ordered to wear the uniform with the camouflage side out unless they were actually fighting in snow-covered terrain. During 1944, a small number of similar garments were made utilising stocks of captured Italian camouflage material. Some of these were reversible and others were lined in fur or sheepskin.

The manufacture of fur-lined items for the Waffen-SS was generally undertaken by the Ostindustrie GmbH and was a speciality of the SS-Bekleidungswerke in the Lublin area, primarily at the Poniatowa and Trawniki labour camps. Fur garments removed from concentration camp inmates throughout the Reich were ordered to be collected and forwarded to Lublin for reprocessing. It is a sad fact that many Waffen-SS soldiers wore winter uniforms lined with fox-furs and stoles taken from old women who had died at Auschwitz, Majdanek, Sobibor and Treblinka.

Plate 94: *A sturdy little 'Jock' of the 51st Highland Division with two somewhat taller Waffen-SS captives in Normandy. The officer in the middle wears the regular motorcyclist's coat. Note also the unofficial attachment of cords to his 'crusher' field cap.* IWM

The SS as a whole placed great emphasis on sport since it served two important purposes, namely keeping SS members fit and building their team spirit. The Waffen-SS was particularly keen to promote athletics as a means of achieving Felix Steiner's goal of producing 'supple, adaptable soldiers capable of far more than average endurance'. Many regional sporting events were organised which pitted various local SS units against one another, and the SS national teams consistently emerged victorious in competitions with their counterparts from the Wehrmacht and the NSDAP paramilitary formations.

The basic SS sports kit comprised a white vest, black shorts, white socks and black shoes. The front of the vest bore a large woven badge featuring black SS runes within a circle. A black vest with white SS runes was also available as an alternative for wear during team events where the opponents would be in white. The SS runes emblem could occasionally be seen on the shorts, which was against regulations, and it was authorised for use by SS doctors who wore it on their white coats. Members of the Leibstandarte had their own shield-shaped sports vest insignia, comprising an eagle's head surmounted by the 'LAH' monogram. A two-piece black tracksuit was issued for 'warming-up' exercises and once again had the SS runes badge on the left breast. Those participating in motorcycle or car racing events wore special green leathers with runes on the jacket and crash helmet, and SS fencers had silver runes within a black diamond stitched to the upper left sleeve of the fencing jacket.

Sportswear was not generally issued to the Waffen-SS after 1941, for reasons of economy, and was thereafter reserved for members of sports teams and for wounded soldiers engaged in exercises and physiotherapy associated with their recuperation.

Plate 95: *Disabled servicemen competing on the games field during their convalescence, 28 March 1942. The man on the right wears SS sports kit.*

95

The standard footwear of the early Armed SS troops comprised two pairs of high marching boots or 'jackboots', one of which was for daily use and the other for dress occasions and parades. From 1934, Leibstandarte non-commissioned personnel were also issued with a pair of the shorter army field service boots, the so-called Knobelbecher or 'dice-shakers', and a pair of lace-up ankle boots for barracks duties. Nearly all new footwear was issued in its natural leather colour and had to be stained and polished by the recipients. Only the best pair of boots was actually bulled, while field boots were simply blackened and left with a dull finish.

Officers generally wore high black riding boots which were privately purchased and so were not of a standard pattern. Some were in stiff leather, others were soft, and a variety of straps and buckles could be employed to prevent the top of the boot from slipping down the calf. A selection of spurs was available for different orders of dress. With walking-out uniform, which included long trousers, officers wore black or patent leather lace-up or elastic-sided ankle boots or shoes.

The first wartime economy measure to hit footwear was the reduction in November 1939 of the height of the shaft of the marching boot from 32cm-41cm to 29cm-35cm, according to size. The distribution of marching boots to replacement and reserve units ceased completely in November 1940, and from July 1942 a standard lace-up ankle boot was issued to most Waffen-SS personnel instead of the marching boot, the continued use of which was restricted to cavalrymen, motorcyclists, engineers and members of guard units. The comfortable new ankle boot was worn with field-grey or olive-green canvas gaiters in winter and puttees in summer. However, the very concept of short boots was hated by the majority of German soldiers, who spoke of 'retreat gaiters' and retained their traditional high marching boots for as long as possible. In fact, the latter made the wearer very prone to developing varicose veins, and many a Waffen-SS infantryman had cause to curse his prized jackboots in later life.

The boots issued to mountain troops had a specially designed lace-up ankle and thick studded soles to aid climbing and skiing. Many alpine officers and even other ranks preferred their own privately purchased footwear, and frequently wore canvas ankle boots with rope or felt soles. In the summer of 1943, the Waffen-SS developed its own style of mountain gaiters based on the old Austrian army 'Styrian' pattern. These were made from various types and colours of leather and canvas, covered the top of the boot like spats, and laced on the outside. Styrian gaiters were widely distributed to the 'Prinz Eugen' and 'Handschar' divisions in the Balkans during 1943-44.

A number of heavy duty items of footwear were devised to combat the subzero temperatures which regularly prevailed on the Eastern Front. These included overboots in compressed and moulded felt, leather, or thick layers of plaited straw. Moreover, rubberised waterproof covers for the feet and legs, originally designed for motorcyclists, were worn by all and sundry in very wet weather or muddy road conditions. During 1944-45 the quality of issue footwear declined dramatically and by the end of the war it was not uncommon to see Waffen-SS soldiers sporting captured enemy footwear, so acute had the leather shortage in Germany become.

In general terms, the Waffen-SS was issued with the same weapons and equipment as the German army during World War 2. This encompassed everything from belt leathers, straps and small arms to mortars, armour and heavy artillery. Initially, ordnance and vehicles were painted field-grey or slate-grey, but by 1943 these shades had proved impractical when used on fronts with differing terrain. Consequently, a dark sand-yellow was universally adopted throughout the Wehrmacht as the standard base colour for metal equipment. During the remainder of the war, tanks, assault guns, panzerfausts and even hand grenades left the factory painted dark yellow, the idea being that a secondary coat of any appropriate camouflage paint could be applied locally as and when circumstances demanded.

A 42mm-wide black leather waist belt, or Koppel, with 1931-pattern SS 'box' buckle in nickel-plated steel or matt grey alloy, was issued to all Waffen-SS NCOs and other ranks and was worn with all orders of dress. Since the belt was traditionally removed for safety reasons when a soldier was placed under close arrest (ie in case he hanged himself with it), its absence came to be regarded as a degradation, and the only non-commissioned personnel allowed out of barracks without wearing their belts were those in military hospitals or who were convalescing. Supporting straps, commonly known as 'Y'-straps, were designed to carry field equipment in conjunction with the belt and were also usually in black leather, although the Waffen-SS experimented with lightweight webbing versions in 1939-40. The SS officer's belt buckle, which was circular in shape, was devised for peacetime use and tended to come undone in action. However, all attempts to modify it were rejected outright by Himmler on the grounds that it had been 'designed by the Führer himself, and made from his own sketches'. As a result, many officers adopted either the sturdier rectangular other ranks' buckle or the basic two-pronged open-face army-pattern buckle when in the field. The officer's cross-strap, an impractical carry-over from the smart prewar years, was discontinued in May 1940 and manufacture of the full-dress woven brocade belt ceased the following year.

Most enlisted personnel in front-line units were armed with 7.92mm Kar.98k rifles and wore two sets of ammunition pouches attached to the belt, each set comprising three compartments holding a total of 30 rounds in six clips. The design of these pouches, or Patronentaschen, dating from 1915, remained virtually unchanged until 1945, although increasing use was made of rivets to replace stitching. NCOs and assault squad leaders issued with MP38s and MP40s sported elongated canvas pouches, each containing three magazines, and similar accessories accompanied the MP28, MP43, MP44 and StG44. Instead

96

Plate 96: *An assault squad of the 'Germania' regiment in France, May 1940. Collar patches have been removed for security reasons, and the men carry smocks folded underneath their belts. A variety of equipment and weaponry is in evidence, including the short-lived SS-pattern webbing supporting straps worn by the man in the centre, who has attached foliage to his steel helmet.*

97

Plate 97: *Heavily armed 'Totenkopf' troops take a meal break during the invasion of the Soviet Union.*

of the right hand ammunition pouch, machine-gunners using the MG34 and MG42 carried a toolcase, or MG-Werkzeugtasche, which held a cleaning kit, spare bolt, ammunition belt, and anti-aircraft sight. The MG42 gunner was also equipped with a spare barrel in a 65cm-long cylindrical container.

The 84/98 bayonet, or Seitengewehr, was standard issue to all German soldiers armed with rifles. It initially had well-finished hardwood grips, but these gave way to bakelite in 1939 and then to poor quality softwood in 1944. The bayonet was carried in a black leather frog, which incorporated

98

a narrow leather grip strap for cavalrymen, and was worn on the left hip suspended from the waist belt. An entrenching tool, or Schanzzeug, comprising a 15cm-wide flat or pointed steel shovel-like blade on a straight wooden handle, was carried in a leather or canvas case, also on the left hip. It was kept in place by a strap which encompassed both the handle and the bayonet sheath when worn together. In 1942, a folding entrenching tool was introduced which could be locked into one of three positions. A special leather and metal case was issued with it, which also provided a useful means of carrying the stick grenade. The Schanzzeug was a formidable close combat weapon, and with the edge of the blade sharpened could virtually decapitate an adversary at a single stroke.

The general issue army gas mask with its fluted cylindrical container was widely distributed to Waffen-SS personnel and officially had to be carried at all times. However, when it quickly became apparent that poison gas was not going to be used by either side during the war, many soldiers jettisoned the mask and used the container for transporting foodstuffs and the occasional clandestine bottle of wine!

The 1934-pattern bread bag, or Brotbeutel, was made of canvas with metal and leather or webbing fittings. It was worn on the right hip suspended from the waist belt, and typically contained eating implements, a small Esbit cooker, washing kit, rifle cleaning tools, needle and thread, and the field cap. An issue water bottle, or Feldflasche, was usually attached by its spring-loaded clip to a D-ring on the bread bag. The 1-litre bottle was at first made of aluminium with a screw cap, then plastic-impregnated wood, and finally enamelled steel with a grey felt cover. The accompanying cup could be in aluminium, steel or plastic and fitted over the screw cap, being held in place by a leather strap. A mess tin, the Kochgeschirr, was normally hung alongside the Feldflasche.

Plate 98: *Waffen-SS infantry advancing through the Ardennes, December 1944. The man in the foreground wearing the camouflage drill tunic is armed with an MP40 and carries the associated ammunition pouches attached to his belt.*

The 1934-pattern back-pack, or Tornister, was made of canvas with leather and metal fittings, and had a cowskin flap. A revised model dating from 1939 had additional D-rings, and during the war some rucksacks were produced with plain canvas flaps. The Tornister was used to carry the drill uniform, underwear, socks, ankle boots, rations and so on, and the Zeltbahn and issue blanket were usually rolled up and placed under the flap. The greatcoat could be strapped across the top and down the sides of the back-pack. A light canvas assault pack, the Sturmgepäck, was designed to hold only the essentials required for a few days' combat use, but was discontinued in 1944.

Map cases, or Meldekartentasche, were issued to almost half of the complete strength of any Waffen-SS unit and were normally worn suspended by two adjustable straps from the waist belt by officers, NCOs and dispatch riders. Service binoculars, or Dienstglas, generally of 6x30 or 10x50 prismatic specification, were also very widely distributed to officers and NCOs, in leather or bakelite cases and with lens covers and button loops. The principal manufacturer was the Jena firm of Carl Zeiss, whose mark often appeared on them. Large numbers of privately-purchased map cases and binoculars were also used.

Pistol holsters were usually bought or issued with their accompanying weapons. The service pistols of the Waffen-SS were the 9mm 'Luger' Parabellum PO8 and the Walther P38, although at the beginning of the war large numbers of obsolete weapons such as the 'broomhandle' Mauser and captured Czech and Polish pistols were frequently carried as well. The preferred officer's sidearm was the handy 7.65mm Walther PPK, which could be purchased from the local SS Kleiderkasse on presentation of the officer's identity papers. According to an order issued by Himmler on 1 January 1943, the pistol had to be worn on the left hip, barrel facing to the back, when in the operational zone and on the right hip, barrel facing to the front, when on home territory (ie when the sword or chained dagger might be worn on the left side). In October 1944, SS officers were instructed to carry loaded pistols at all times when in public, and reminded to take extra care to ensure that they were not stolen when frequenting railway stations, dance halls and the like.

The short fighting knife or Kampfmesser, dating from 1914, evolved into a number of distinct patterns and many types co-existed during World War 2. The issue model predominated in the Waffen-SS and was made of steel with a brown wooden grip and black metal scabbard. The latter featured a spring steel clip which could be attached to the top of the marching boot, or to the front of the tunic or camouflage smock at chest level.

In addition to the foregoing, there were several other items of personal equipment commonly carried by the Waffen-SS. A variety of small box-like field torches were produced, with integral leather tabs so that they could be hung from tunic or overcoat buttons. These generally had red, green and blue coloured filters for use in signalling. Goggles, compasses, pencils, maps, prescribed spectacles and a host of other sundries including tobacco, cigarettes and condoms were widely distributed, while cavalrymen, engineers and mountain troops had their own specialist items like saddle-bags, machetes and ice picks. On a cord around the neck, every SS soldier wore an oval zinc identity disc which was divided in half by perforated holes and bore details of his service number, unit and blood group (the latter also being tattooed under his arm). In the event of death, the disc was broken in half, the portion on the cord remaining with the body and the other half being taken away for recording purposes.

99

Many hundreds of proof and makers' codes, the so-called 'Waffenamt stamps', were used by the government inspectorates and manufacturers of small arms, ammunition and equipment during the Third Reich. These codes were altered from time to time for security reasons, and large firms were allocated several marks simultaneously. A small but representative selection of the most common codes is given below.

Code	***Firm***	***Product***
ac	Carl Walther, Zella-Mehlis	Small Arms
amn	Mauser Werke AG, Waldeck	Small Arms
amo	Mauser Werke AG, Neuwied	Small Arms
ar	Mauser Werke AG, Berlin	Small Arms
ayf	Waffenfabrik 'Erma', Erfurt	Small Arms
blc	Carl Zeiss, Jena	Optics
bml	Hans Romer, Neu-Ulm	Holsters
bvl	Theodor Bergmann AG, Hamburg	Small Arms
byf	Mauser Werke AG, Oberndorf	Small Arms
cag	Swarovski & Co, Tyrol	Optics
cdo	Theodor Bergmann AG, Veltem	Small Arms
cdp	Theodor Bergmann AG, Berlin	Small Arms
ce	Sauer & Sohn, Suhl	Holsters
cof	Carl Eickhorn, Solingen	Bayonets
cra	Paul Weyersberg, Solingen	Bayonets
cul	WKC Waffenfabrik, Solingen	Bayonets
cvl	WKC Waffenfabrik, Solingen	Bayonets
dpv	Carl Zeiss, Dresden	Optics
dpw	Carl Zeiss, Berlin	Optics
dpx	Carl Zeiss, Stuttgart	Optics
emq	Carl Zeiss, Jena	Optics
fxo	C.G. Haenel, Suhl	Small Arms
gsc	S.A. Belge, Monceau	Ammunition
gug	Ungarische Optische Werke, Budapest	Optics
hhg	Rheinmetall-Borsig AG, Berlin	Artillery
jfp	Carl Zeiss, Berlin	Optics
kfg	Yugoslavian State Arsenal, Sarajevo	Ammunition
kls	Steyr-Daimler Puch AG, Warsaw	Small Arms
ksb	Manufacture Nationale d'Armes, Paris	Small Arms
kza	Mauser Werke AG, Karlsruhe	Small Arms
lmg	Carl Zeiss, Jena	Optics
mrb	Aktiengesellschaft, Prague	Small Arms
pcd	Theodor Bergmann AG, Berlin	Small Arms
qve	Carl Walther, Zella-Mehlis	Small Arms
rln	Carl Zeiss, Jena	Optics
svw	Mauser Werke AG, Oberndorf	Small Arms

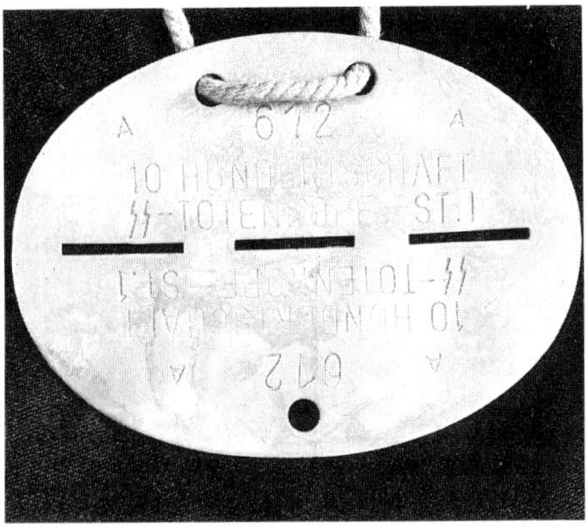

Plate 99: *A zinc identity disc bearing details of the wearer's blood group, service number and unit, ie 'A 612 : 10 Hundertschaft SS-Totenkopf-St. 1'.*

4 Waffen-SS Insignia

MANUFACTURE AND SUPPLY

While the majority of wartime Waffen-SS uniforms were made by SS-owned economic enterprises, the insignia attached to them always tended to be manufactured by long established private companies. That arrangement necessitated strict standardisation and quality control, the administration of which was entrusted to the Reichszeugmeisterei or RZM, a body which had been set up as early as 1 April 1929 to supervise the production and pricing of all Nazi Party uniform items. The basic functions of the RZM were to see that NSDAP contracts went to Aryan firms and to ensure that final products were of a high standard yet priced to suit the pocket of the average Party member. It also acted as a 'clearing house' between manufacturers on the one hand and wholesalers and retailers on the other. On 16 March 1935, contract numbers were introduced and awarded to every RZM-approved company, and after that date RZM numbers replaced makers' marks on all NSDAP accoutrements. So the buttons, belt hooks, etc of the Allgemeine-SS, which always remained an organ of the Nazi Party, consistently featured RZM marks. Those members of the Waffen-SS, however, which was in effect a State arm during World War 2, very seldom did.

Waffen-SS insignia fell into several distinct categories, according to manufacture. Each of these will now be described in turn.

Metal badges such as eagles and death's heads for the peaked cap, totenkopf buttons for the 1934-pattern field cap, shoulder strap cyphers and rank pips were made in a variety of materials, dependent primarily upon date of production. The most common combinations were as follows:

1. Plated brass (1933-36)
2. Plated tombakbronze (1933-36)
3. Copper-plated aluminium with a surface wash (1936-45)
4. Bare aluminium (1936-45)
5. Plated steel (1939-45)
6. Painted steel (1939-45)
7. Plated zinc (1942-45)
8. Painted zinc (1942-45)
9. Bare zinc (1944-45)

In general terms the quality of metals used declined as the war progressed, but despite that, a good standard of overall finish and appearance was always maintained. Early to midwar examples were usually crisply die-struck, with hollow backs bearing two or three flat prongs or round pins for attachment purposes. The reverse of these items tended to feature a mirror image of the obverse design. Late-war badges were often cast, with smooth concave backs.

Cap eagles and death's heads, which were common to both the Allgemeine-SS and Waffen-SS, normally bore RZM marks, either individually stamped on to the badge reverse or embossed into it as part of the die-striking or casting process. Typical examples were 'RZM M1/52' (Deschler & Sohn of Munich) and 'RZM M1/167' (Augustin Hicke of Tyssa bei Bodenbach). During the war, the format of RZM codes used on metal SS insignia changed, deleting the 'M1' prefix and adding a year suffix, eg 'RZM 499/41'. No list of these later codes is known to have survived, and so they have never been deciphered.

The earliest SS cloth badges were hand-embroidered, and this form of insignia was worn by soldiers of the Armed SS during the 1933-35 period. Hand-embroidery could be in white or silver-grey cotton thread, fine aluminium wire or heavy silver bullion, with the latter two styles normally being reserved for officers. However, in September 1934 non-commissioned and enlisted ranks of the LAH and the new SS-VT were also authorised to wear aluminium wire insignia with the black uniform, to set them apart from their colleagues in the Allgemeine-SS. No two hand-embroidered badges were ever identical, since they were individually made. The embroidery was usually done over cardboard templates, which comprised thin cutouts of the relevant designs and which could vary slightly from one maker to another. Once the actual embroidery was completed, a paper or cloth backing was glued on to the reverse of each piece to prevent fraying. Badge companies generally employed women to do this work, or farmed it out to local seamstresses on a cottage industry basis.

In 1936, by which time the RZM had become effectively organised under Reichszeugmeister Richard Büchner, machine-embroidered insignia began to be produced and widely distributed for wear by SS enlisted men and NCOs. This form of embroidery was cheap and quick to execute, and generally utilised white or silver-grey cotton thread on a black woven badgecloth base. The thickness of the embroidery depended on how the individual manufacturer's machine was adjusted, but it usually had a tightly-formed and raised appearance. The only exception was the flat chain-stitch embroidery which was sometimes employed on shoulder strap badges. The producers of machine-embroidered insignia were normally fairly substantial firms, as only they could afford the expensive equipment involved in the manufacturing process. Such companies were rigidly controlled by the RZM, and their products had to carry labels bearing the relevant contract numbers. In addition to the standard RZM paper tags used by all NSDAP formations, a system of small black and white woven labels was devised specifically for SS items. Each bore the RZM symbol and SS runes together with the maker's contract number and year date, an example being 'RZM 21/36 SS'. Where a firm was engaged only in embroidery work the letters 'St' denoting 'Stickerei' or 'embroiderer', were incorporated into the label, for example "RZM St 459/36 SS'. It was not uncommon for two such labels to be attached to a single badge, particularly a cuff title, if two separate firms were involved in its manufacture due to sub-contracting. One label would refer to the maker of the backing and the other to the embroiderer. Because of the foregoing, machine-embroidered insignia has come to be known as the 'RZM-style' by collectors.

Machine-woven badges were produced from 1939, using artificial silk and either cotton or fine aluminium wire. They had a very flat appearance and the manufacturing process, which could result in hundreds of identical insignia being run off on a single continuous strip of ribbon-like material, allowed for the incorporation of very fine detail into the design. The principal producer of these badges was the Wuppertal-Barmen firm of Bandfabrik Ewald Vorsteher, whose trademark 'BEVO' has come to be used when referring to all machine-woven insignia.

The use of silk-screen printing in the manufacture of certain Waffen-SS badges was introduced in 1944 but was primarily restricted to foreign volunteer shields, war auxiliary armbands and the special rank insignia for camouflage clothing. Cheap production costs were more than outweighed by the poor quality of the finished article, and printed badges were very unpopular.

The procedures governing the approval and manufacture of Waffen-SS insignia were very complicated. Various SS departments, particularly the SS Hauptamt (SS-HA), the SS Führungshauptamt (SS-FHA) and the SS Wirtschafts- und Verwaltungshauptamt (SS-WVHA) were continually at each other's throats over who was responsible for this matter, and the process by which new badges were proposed and introduced was eventually settled in May 1944, as follows:

- The SS-HA became primarily responsible for the design and proposal to the Reichsführer-SS of 'political' SS insignia, ie, national emblems, collar patches, arm shields and formation badges. However, the SS-HA had first to get the opinion of the SS-FHA before submitting samples to the Reichsführer.

100

Plate 100: *A selection of Waffen-SS insignia. These are:*

A 1943-pattern horizontal death's head collar patch, BEVO machine-woven in silver-grey cotton.

B SS runes, or Sig-runes, collar patch machine-embroidered in silver-grey cotton.

C 1938-pattern arm eagle with curved head, machine-embroidered in silver-grey cotton c1942-43.

D Vertical 'death's head/13' collar patch, hand-embroidered in aluminium wire.

E Rank collar patch for an SS-Untersturmführer.

Plate 101: *Reverse views of the insignia shown in Plate 100. Note the typical RZM paper label affixed to the pre-1940 'death's head/13' collar patch. Such labels did not appear on later wartime patches.*

101

- The SS-FHA became primarily responsible for the design and proposal to the Reichsführer-SS of 'non-political' insignia, ie rank badges, cuff titles, qualification badges, branch of service insignia and specialist badges. If political considerations arose in respect of any of these, the SS-FHA had to obtain the opinion of the SS-HA before submission to the Reichsführer.
- The SS-HA would, after obtaining the approval of the Reichsführer, cede badges listed in the first paragraph above to the SS-FHA. The SS-FHA was then responsible for the execution and issue of the badges in co-operation with the SS-WVHA. The SS-FHA and SS-WVHA would collaborate until the completion of final samples of these badges.
- The method of wearing new types of badges would be decided in relation to the method of wearing existing badges. If changes in the method of wear were necessary, the SS-FHA was responsible for making them. However, if insignia mentioned in the first paragraph above were involved, the SS-FHA had to obtain the opinion of the SS-HA first.

To complicate the issue still further, Himmler himself also suggested the introduction of special badges, such as cuff titles for as yet unnamed SS regiments and divisions. He was personally responsible for some designs, and often consulted with two artists on his Persönlicher Stab, namely SS-Oberführer Professor Benno von Arent and SS-Oberführer Professor Karl Diebitsch. Once a design had been approved by the Reichsführer it would pass to the SS-WVHA which would in turn authorise the RZM to supply the required quantity. The RZM then placed a contract with one of its approved firms and the finished badges were delivered to one of the SS clothing depots, usually Dachau, from where they would finally be supplied to the unit concerned. So, in the production of a single new badge, no less than four departments, ie the SS-HA, SS-FHA, SS-WVHA and Hauptamt Persönlicher Stab RfSS might, and probably would, be involved!

By September 1944, pressures on the RZM had developed to such an extent that it was forced to terminate its involvement in the supply of insignia to the Waffen-SS. The following December it announced that Waffen-SS eagles, death's heads, collar patches, shoulder straps and cuff titles could henceforth be manufactured, without a contract, for direct sale to authorised wholesalers and retailers for the duration of the war. By that stage, no less than 24 firms were producing cloth insignia for the Waffen-SS. These companies are listed below:

Gebrüder Auerhammer, Weissenburg
Albrecht Bender, Weissenburg
Max Dörfel, Eibenstock
Lothar von Dreden & Co, Wuppertal-Elberfeld
Oskar Frank, Eibenstock
Geissler & Hast, Ansbach
August Göbels Söhne, Gross-Schönau
E. Günther, Eibenstock
Hensel & Schuhmann, Berlin
Hinterleitner, Brunnacker & Co, Weissenburg
E. Köhler, Annaberg
Kruse & Söhne, Wuppertal-Barmen
Sigmund Lendvay, Vienna
Lucas & Vorsteher, Wuppertal-Barmen
F. Müller, Rossbach
R. Nitzsche, Eibenstock
J.F. Rieleder, Heilbronn
Julius Riess, Erfurt
Franz Rönnefahrt, Brandenburg
Hermann Schmuck & Co, Weissenburg
Thiele & Steinert, Freiberg
Tröltsch & Hanselmann, Berlin
Ewald Vorsteher, Wuppertal-Barmen
Ferdinand Winter, Treuchtlingen

102

Plate 102: *Machine-embroidered cuff title and arm shield of the Flemish Legion.*

THE WAFFENFARBE SYSTEM

During the Third Reich, certain colours were employed in the design of military, paramilitary and civil uniforms, and accoutrements, as a methodical means of unit identification. These colours appeared on tunic facings, cap piping, armbands and so on and were known as branch of service colours or 'Waffengattungsfarben', normally referred to in the abbreviated form 'Waffenfarbe'.

Before the outbreak of World War 2, all Armed SS piping was white, silver or twisted black and silver, like that of the Allgemeine-SS. However, in December 1939, due to the increasing militarisation of the Waffen-SS and its new-found associations with Wehrmacht forces, shoulder straps piped in army Waffenfarbe were introduced. A few officers also began to equip themselves with Waffenfarbe-piped peaked caps and long trousers, made to order through their local Kleiderkasse, but Himmler immediately forbade that practice, instructing that the piping on these items was to remain white. Some confusion then ensued, for in May 1940 the Reichsführer backtracked by indicating that peaked caps could thereafter be piped in Waffenfarbe, although all walking-out dress trousers were now to be piped in grey. The following November Himmler changed his mind yet again, directing that Waffenfarbe was once more to be restricted to shoulder straps and the soutache on the field cap, with all other piping reverting to white or aluminium depending on rank. It is clear that the Reichsführer wanted his soldiers to retain their unique appearance, distinct from that of the army, but a number of Waffen-SS officers and men continued to wear Waffenfarbe on their peaked caps until the end of the war, in defiance of Himmler's orders.

The following table shows the Waffenfarbe colours which were officially authorised for use by the Waffen-SS branches listed at various stages during World War 2. However, it should be noted that a few shades were withdrawn, reallocated or even renamed from time to time, and in any case the differences in some colours were so slight as to be almost indistinguishable, a situation compounded by variations in manufacturers' dyes, the bleaching effect of the sun and the general weathering of piping under field conditions. The result of all this is that there is often heated debate between buyers and sellers of surviving piped items as to whether the Waffenfarbe colours concerned are rare or relatively common ones.

Waffenfarbe		***Waffen-SS Branch of Service***
BLACK		Construction Units Engineers
BLUE	*(i) Dark (or 'Cornflower') Blue*	Medical
	(ii) Light Blue	Field Post Office (from February 1943) Motor Technical School (until July 1942) Supply Transport (until August 1944)
	(iii) Sky Blue	Administration
BROWN	*(i) Copper Brown*	Reconnaissance (until June 1942)
	(ii) Light Brown	Concentration Camps

Waffenfarbe		***Waffen-SS Branch of Service***
GREEN	*(i) Dark Green*	Reserve Officers (discontinued 1942) Specialists (until June 1942)
	(ii) Grass Green	Mountain Troops (from May 1942) Police-Division (discontinued 1942)
GREY	*(i) Light Grey*	General Officers Himmler's Staff (until June 1942)
	(ii) Dark Grey	Himmler's Staff (from June 1942)
ORANGE		Field Police Garrison Troops Motor Technical School (from July 1942 until August 1944) Recruiting Technical Units Welfare
PINK	*(i) Light Pink*	Motor Technical School (from August 1944) Transport (from August 1944)
	(ii) Rose Pink	Anti-tank troops Panzer
	(iii) Salmon Pink	Military Geologists
RED	*(i) Bright Red*	Artillery Flak Rocket Units
	(ii) Claret (or Bordeaux) Red	Legal Service
	(iii) Crimson Red	Veterinary
RED & GREY TWIST		Specialists (from June 1942)
WHITE		Infantry
YELLOW	*(i) Golden Yellow*	Cavalry Reconnaissance (from June 1942)
	(ii) Lemon Yellow	Field Post Office (until February 1943) Signals War Correspondents

The Waffen-SS rank structure developed as the organisation expanded. The definitive format, dating from April 1942, is shown below. Non-German nationals from Germanic countries serving in foreign legions raised by the SS replaced the rank prefix 'SS-' with 'Legions-' (eg, 'Legions-Hauptsturmführer') while those in non-Germanic units used the prefix 'Waffen-' (eg 'Waffen-Hauptsturmführer der SS'). This denoted their attachment to, rather than membership of, the SS.

Mannschaften (Other Ranks)

- SS-Schütze — Private
- SS-Oberschütze — Private (after 6 months' service)
- SS-Sturmmann — Lance Corporal
- SS-Rottenführer — Senior Lance Corporal

Unterführer ohne Portepee (Junior NCOs)

- SS-Unterscharführer — Corporal
- SS-Scharführer — Sergeant

Unterführer mit Portepee (Senior NCOs)

- SS-Oberscharfürher — Staff Sergeant
- SS-Hauptscharführer — Sergeant-Major
- SS-Sturmscharführer — Company Sergeant-Major

(Men holding any of the above five Unterführer ranks could be appointed to serve as their unit's SS-Stabsscharführer or 'Duty NCO', who fulfilled various administrative and reporting functions. The Stabsscharführer was nicknamed 'der Spiess' or 'the spear', a traditional term dating back to pikemen of the Middle Ages.)

Untere Führer (Company Officers)

- SS-Untersturmführer — 2nd Lieutenant
- SS-Obersturmführer — Lieutenant
- SS-Hauptsturmführer — Captain

Mittlere Führer (Field Officers)

- SS-Sturmbannführer — Major
- SS-Obersturmbannführer — Lieutenant-Colonel
- SS-Standartenführer — Colonel
- SS-Oberführer — Senior Colonel

Höhere Führer (General Officers)

- SS-Brigadeführer und Generalmajor der Waffen-SS — Brigadier-General
- SS-Gruppenführer und Generalleutnant der Waffen-SS — Major-General
- SS-Obergruppenführer und General der Waffen-SS — Lieutenant-General
- SS-Oberst-Gruppenführer und Generaloberst der Waffen-SS — General

(All Waffen-SS Generals were awarded their corresponding army rank titles, eg, Generalmajor in 1940. From 1943, police Generals who had commanded Waffen-SS field formations were allowed to incorporate 'Waffen-SS' into their titles, eg 'SS-Obergruppenführer und General der Waffen-SS und Polizei', and the same all-embracing designation was given to each of the HSSPfs in 1944. The latter were technically responsible for all SS formations, including Waffen-SS units, based in their territories.)

While the day-to-day tactical command of most Waffen-SS units was devolved to Wehrmacht Generals during the war, Himmler retained his overall authority as Reichsführer-SS. Hitler himself was ultimately Commander-in-Chief of the entire armed forces and SS and held the personal titles of 'Der Oberste Befehlshaber der Wehrmacht' and 'Der Oberste Führer der Schutzstaffel'.

The regular Waffen-SS officer candidate or Führerbewerber (FB), distinguished by a double lace bar on his shoulder straps, underwent four months' basic training after

FIG 13

Dienstrangabzeichen der Waffen-SS

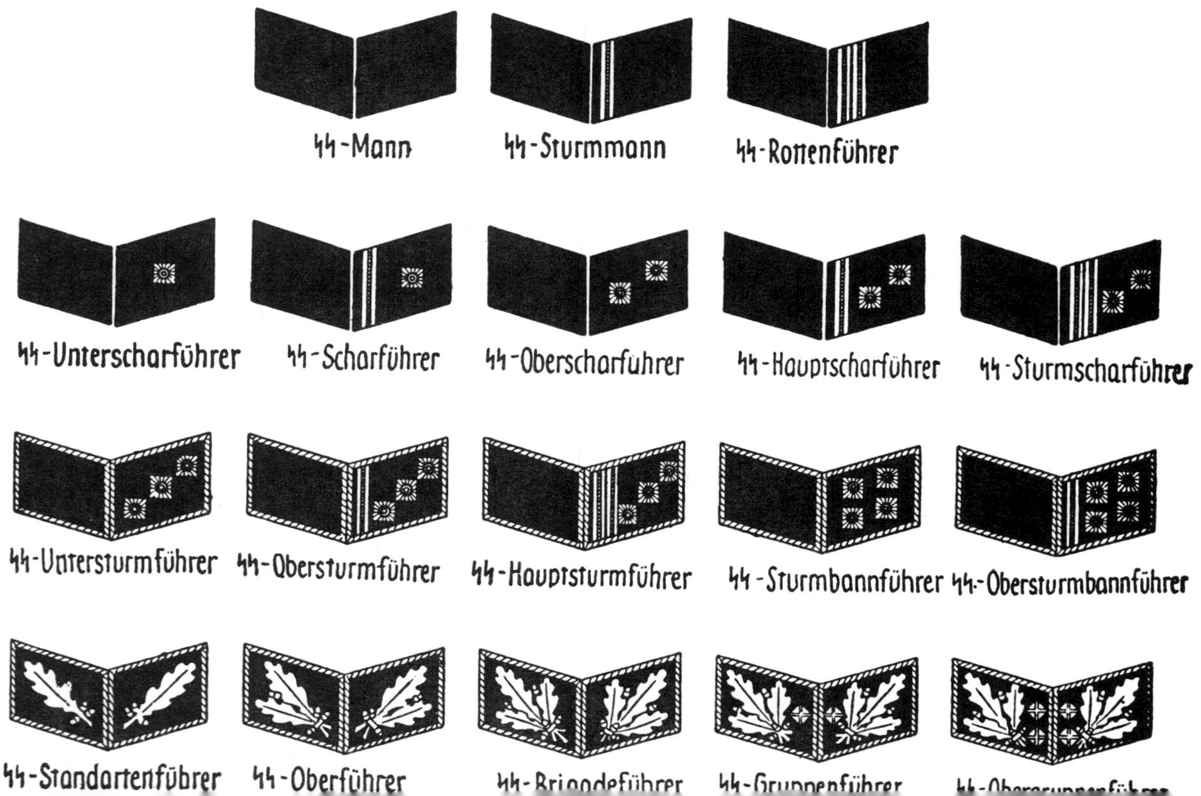

SS-Mann SS-Sturmmann SS-Rottenführer

SS-Unterscharführer SS-Scharführer SS-Oberscharführer SS-Hauptscharführer SS-Sturmscharführer

SS-Untersturmführer SS-Obersturmführer SS-Hauptsturmführer SS-Sturmbannführer SS-Obersturmbannführer

SS-Standartenführer SS-Oberführer SS-Brigadeführer SS-Gruppenführer SS-Obergruppenführer

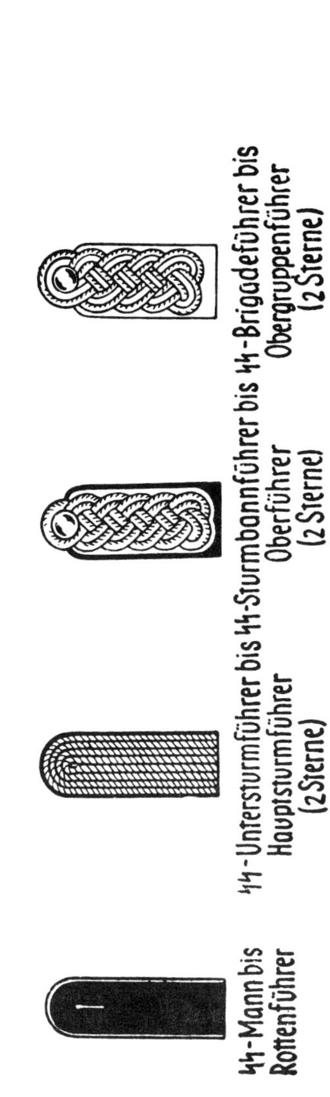

Fig 13: *1942-pattern SS rank insignia as worn on collar patches and shoulder straps. For ranks below Standartenführer, the blank right-hand collar patch would normally sport the SS runes, death's head or some other unit symbol.*

which he became an officer cadet or Führeranwärter (FA) and received the title of SS-Junker with the equivalent rank of SS-Unterscharführer. He then attended a six-month military leadership course which culminated in his promotion to SS-Standartenjunker, equal to an SS-Scharführer. At the end of a further six months' officer training he was elevated to the position of SS-Standartenoberjunker, equating to an SS-Hauptscharführer, and was allowed to wear officer's cap cords, belt buckle and aluminium collar patch piping. He was then sent back to his unit where, after a minimum period of two months, he received promotion to SS-Untersturmführer. Officers who did not plan a military career and intended to serve in the Waffen-SS only for the duration of the war were given reserve commissions and were known as Reserve-Führerbewerber (RFB), Reserve-Führeranwärter (RFA), SS-Junker der Reserve, and so on.

Potential NCOs, or SS-Unterführerbewerber, were generally trained at a company level, progressing to SS-Unterführeranwärter and then to SS-Unterscharführer. During their training, they wore a single lace bar on their shoulder straps if they had signed up for 12 years' service or more, and a thin twisted cord in the appropriate Waffenfarbe if they had signed up for less than 12 years.

The Waffen-SS also employed civilian specialists (interpreters, doctors and so on) known as Sonderführer, and later Fachführer, who were given appointments in relation to their tasks. They could hold the ranks of:

- SS-Unterscharführer (S) or (F)
- SS-Hauptscharführer (S) or (F)
- SS-Untersturmführer (S) or (F)
- SS-Hauptsturmführer (S) or (F)
- SS-Sturmbannführer (S) or (F)

The SS-Fachführer wore a blank right collar patch and shoulder strap piping in dark green until June 1942. After that date, piping was a red/grey twist. If a specialist showed that he was capable of commanding a military unit corresponding to his Fachführer rank, the latter ceased and he continued in his duties as a full officer or NCO of the Waffen-SS.

FIG 14

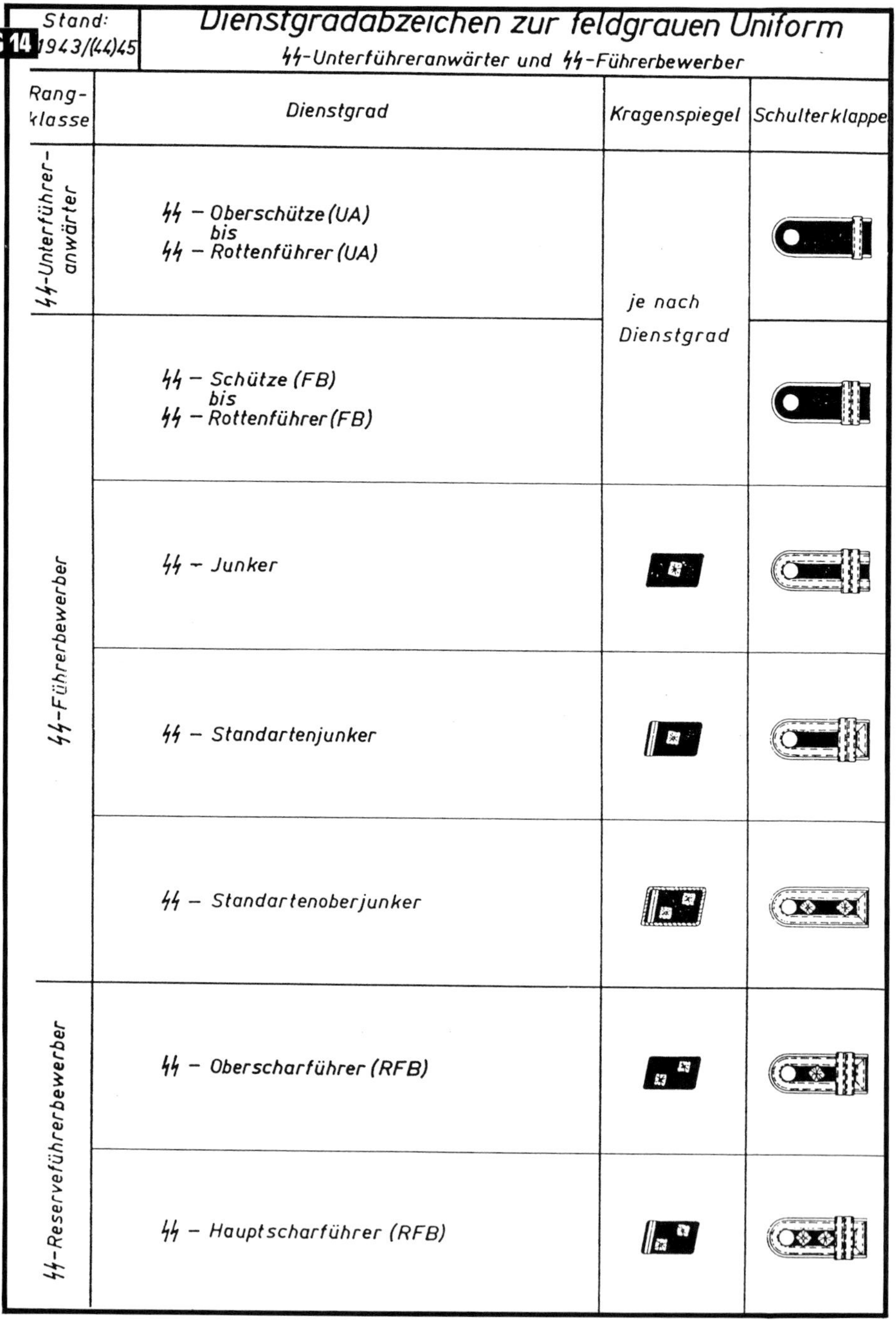

Stand: 1943/(44)45	Dienstgradabzeichen zur feldgrauen Uniform ϟϟ-Unterführeranwärter und ϟϟ-Führerbewerber		
Rangklasse	**Dienstgrad**	**Kragenspiegel**	**Schulterklappe**
ϟϟ-Unterführeranwärter	ϟϟ – Oberschütze (UA) bis ϟϟ – Rottenführer (UA)	je nach Dienstgrad	
ϟϟ-Führerbewerber	ϟϟ – Schütze (FB) bis ϟϟ – Rottenführer (FB)		
	ϟϟ – Junker		
	ϟϟ – Standartenjunker		
	ϟϟ – Standartenoberjunker		
ϟϟ-Reserveführerbewerber	ϟϟ – Oberscharführer (RFB)		
	ϟϟ – Hauptscharführer (RFB)		

Fig 14: *Rank insignia worn by Waffen-SS officer candidates and potential NCOs. Note the distinctive lace bars across the shoulder straps, and officer's piping on the Standartenoberjunker collar patch.*

FIG 15

Stand: 1943/45	Dienstgradabzeichen an Tarn- und Schutzanzügen SS-Führer	
Rang-klasse	Dienstgrad	Ärmelabzeichen
SS-Führer	SS-Untersturmführer	
	SS-Obersturmführer	
	SS-Hauptsturmführer	
	SS-Sturmbannführer	
	SS-Obersturmbannführer	
	SS-Standartenführer	
	SS-Oberführer	
	SS-Brigadeführer u. Generalmajor d. Waffen-SS	
	SS-Gruppenführer u. Generalleutnant d. Waffen-SS	
	SS-Obergruppenführer u. General d. Waffen-SS	
	SS-Oberstgruppenführer u. Generaloberst d. Waffen-SS	

Fig 15: *1943-pattern rank insignia for wearby officers on camouflage clothing. Badges for Oberführer and below were in green on black, whilst those for Brigadeführer and above were in yellow on black.*

The first SS collar patches, or Kragenspiegel, were introduced in August 1929 and were based on those of the SA. Like their successors, early examples were black and featured rank insignia on the left patch, or both patches for Standartenführer and above, with unit designations on the right. However, they were far from formalised and were sometimes even 'home-made'. Sizes and shapes differed considerably and the attendant numerals, pips, bars and oakleaves varied in construction from crude white or grey embroidery to fine silver wire and a whole range of metals. By 1932, SS collar patches had become fairly standardised at about 40mm x 55mm, and their production was limited to contracted manufacturers. Patches for Standartenführer and above were thereafter universally made of black velvet, while those for lower ranks were in a woven artificial velvet or woollen badgecloth, folded over a cardboard or canvas base.

The earliest Armed SS units were technically on the local Abschnitte staff, and as such members wore blank right collar patches. In May 1933, officers' patches began to be piped in a black/aluminium twisted cord, and those of other ranks in white cord. With the rapid expansion of the militarised SS formations, it soon became clear that some kind of distinctive collar insignia was required for the Leibstandarte and Politische Bereitschaften, and towards the end of the year patches bearing double Sig-Runes, hand-embroidered in silver bullion for officers and white or silver-grey cotton for other ranks, were issued to soldiers of the LAH. In June 1934, the SS PBs attached to Oberabschnitte Süd, Südwest and Mitte were authorised to wear runic 'SS 1', 'SS 2' and 'SS 3' patches respectively, with the numbers as large as the runes, and three months later non-commissioned ranks in the LAH and newly-constituted SS-VT were further distinguished by being allowed to use aluminium wire embroidery on their collar patches. In October, the piping on officers' patches was changed to the definitive plain aluminium cord, with the black/aluminium twist now being adopted by other ranks.

The rest of the prewar period witnessed the introduction of machine-embroidered collar patches for the field uniform, death's heads and other designs for SS-TV and specialist units, and the adoption of the 'SS 1', 'SS 2', and 'SS 3' patches, this time with small numbers, by the 'Deutschland', 'Germania' and 'Der Führer' Standarten. Some collar patches were produced on metal bases with screw fittings at each corner, so they could be easily removed from the tunic when it was being cleaned.

When army-pattern shoulder straps were introduced for the Armed SS in March 1938, it was apparent that the wearing of dual rank badges on both the left collar patch (SS rank) and shoulder straps (army equivalent) was unnecessary. However, Himmler decreed that SS ranks should still be displayed. The situation was exacerbated at the outbreak of war, with the LAH, SS-VT and SS-TV being given specific roles alongside the Wehrmacht.

103

Plate 103: *The ubiquitous wartime SS runes collar patch. This example is hand-embroidered in aluminium wire, but all officially issued runic patches produced during the 1940-45 period were identical in configuration, irrespective of their method of construction. Patches with larger runes, or with runes lying at a different angle, must be viewed with suspicion.*

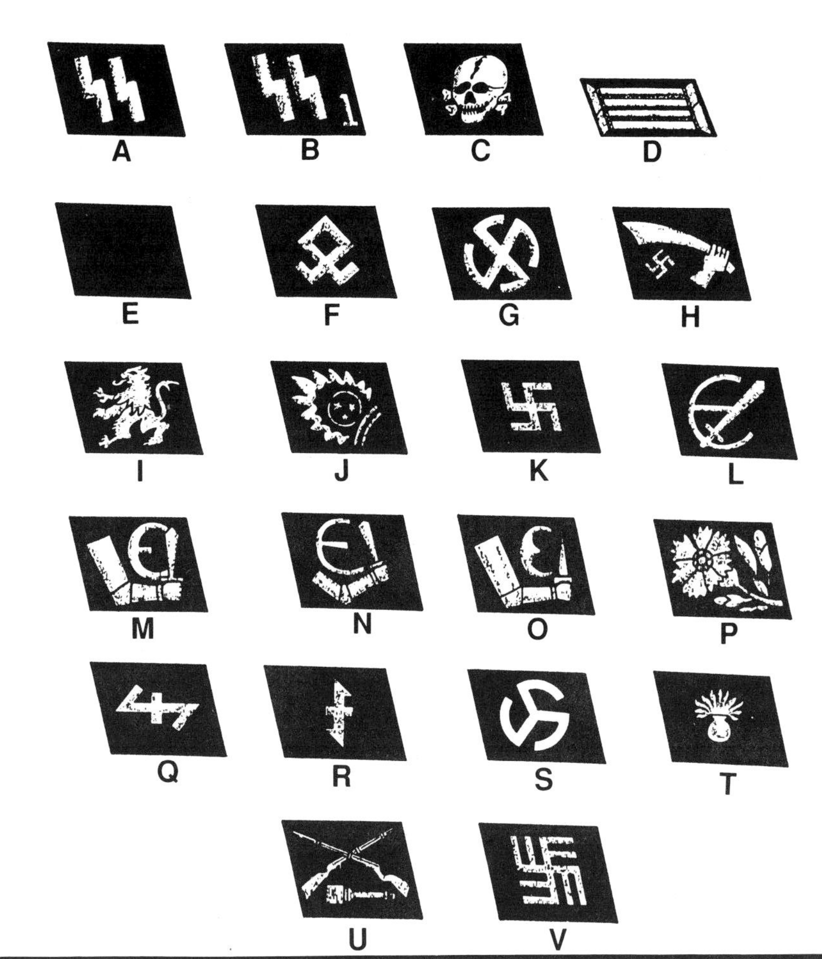

Fig 16: *A selection of Waffen-SS collar patches known to have been issued and worn by the following units during World War 2:*

- *A* *All German and Germanic Waffen-SS formations*
- *B* *SS-VT Standarte 'Deutschland'*
- *C* *Totenkopf units*
- *D* *SS-Polizei-Division and SS-Polizei Regiments*
- *E* *Specialists and foreign units not allocated other patches*
- *F* *'Prinz Eugen'*
- *G* *'Nordland'*
- *H* *'Handschar'*
- *I* *14th Division*
- *J* *15th Division*
- *K* *Latvian Legion/15th and 19th Divisions*
- *L* *20th Division (official patch dating from June 1944)*
- *M* *20th Division (unofficial patch dating from October 1943)*
- *N* *20th Division (official patch dating from October 1944)*
- *O* *20th Division (unofficial patch made in Tartu, February 1944)*
- *P* *'Maria Theresa'*
- *Q* *Dutch Legion/'Nederland' (official patch dating from November 1941)*
- *R* *Dutch Legion/'Nederland' (unofficial patch)*
- *S* *'Nordwest'/Freikorps Danmakr/Flemish Legion/'Langemarck'*
- *T* *'Landstorm Nederland' (unofficially continued from the Landwacht Nederland)*
- *U* *Dirlewanger Brigade/36th Division*
- *V* *Non-SS concentration camp guards*

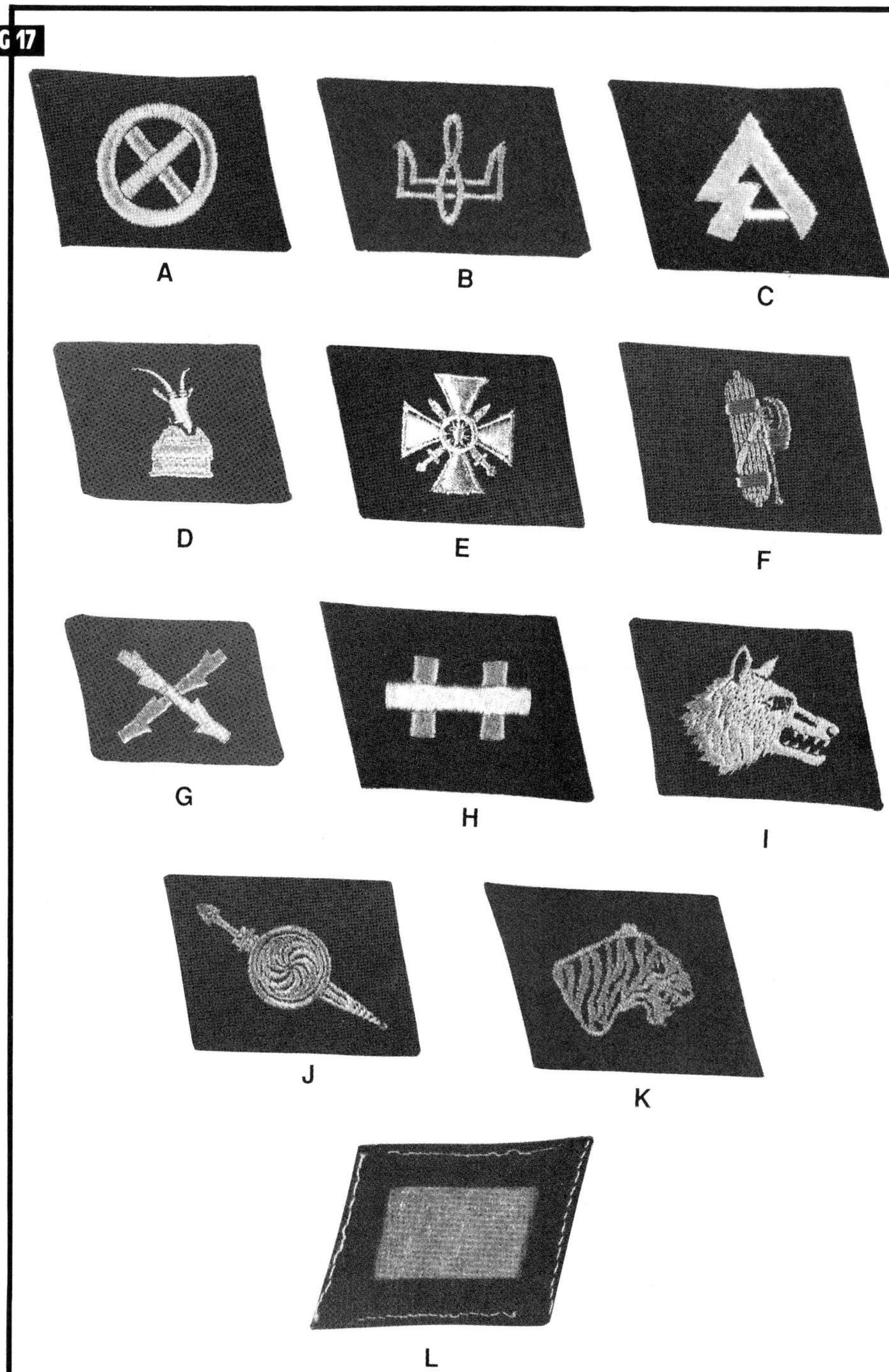
FIG 17
A
B
C
D
E
F
G
H
I
J
K
L

Fig 17: *Designs of some alleged Waffen-SS collar patches, several of which are said to have been discovered in the Dachau clothing store in April 1945. These must be regarded with the utmost suspicion as their existence prior to the end of the war has not been confirmed. Many of these designs are based on illustrations forming part of a dubious so-called 'SS-Hauptamt Map' dated February 1945, which purports to show projected collar patches and arm shields for new Waffen-SS units. The authenticity of the map itself has never been proven.*

A Closed sonnenrad
B Trident of Vladimir
C SA Rune
D Goat's head helmet
E Cross of St George
F Fasces
G Cross of Burgundy
H Russian Orthodox Cross
I Wolf's head
J Sword and shield
K Tiger's head
L Reverse of a 'Dachau patch', showing the distinctive grey-white thread border characteristic of this series of badges.

The ordinary German soldier was bemused by the SS rank system and was at a loss to know which SS men he was supposed to salute and whose orders he was obliged to obey. It therefore became absolutely essential, for practical and disciplinary reasons, that Waffen-SS rank badges should correspond to those in the armed forces and be easily recognised as such. Consequently, during the formation of the first SS field divisions in the autumn of 1939, it was decided that their personnel should not wear SS rank patches. Instead, they received matching collar patches with the runes or death's head on both sides. Their ranks were indicated solely by shoulder straps, in the army style. However, prewar Waffen-SS officers and men jealously retained their existing collar patches, showing their SS ranks.

The increased use of camouflage smocks, which covered the shoulder straps and, indeed, all insignia except the collar patches, led Himmler to rescind the matching collar patch order on 10 May 1940 and reintroduce the SS rank patch for all Waffen-SS members. At the same time the need for security during the invasion of the Low Countries and France rendered obsolete all SS-VT and SS-TV collar patches bearing numerals or letters, which were ordered removed. The result was that for a short time during the Western campaign personnel in the SS-Verfügungsdivision wore no collar patches at all. From then on, the basic SS runes collar patch became standard for all German and Germanic Waffen-SS formations except Totenkopf units, whose members continued to wear the death's head, now produced in a horizontal version more suitable for use on the closed-neck field tunic. In August 1940, the black/aluminium twisted cord bordering other ranks' patches was abolished, leaving

Plate 104: *Alfred Wünnenberg wearing the police litzen collar patches used by the Polizei-Division between 1939 and 1942. This photograph is also interesting for its portrayal of the common wartime press ploy of 'touching up' old pictures to update them for propaganda reasons. Wünnenberg won the Knight's Cross on 15 November 1941 as a police Oberst at Leningrad, and that is when this photograph was originally taken. On 23 April 1942 he was awarded the Oakleaves as an SS-Brigadeführer, and for the purposes of an immediate press announcement the old photo was dragged out of the files and had the Oakleaves painted on. This type of alteration can often be seen in surviving press photographs and extends to rank badges as well as decorations.*

104

105

Plate 105: *Sepp Dietrich wearing his collar patches as SS-Oberst-Gruppenführer und Panzer Generaloberst der Waffen-SS, the senior active tank man at the front. Although promoted to this rank on 20 April 1942, Wehrmacht pressure prevented him from adopting the appropriate insignia until he had secured command of a suitably large force, which he did in the autumn of 1944 with the formation of the 6th SS-Panzer Army.*

Plate 106: *When the British liberated Belsen concentration camp on 17 April 1945, they found it staffed largely by wounded and recuperating officers and men who had been transferred in on a temporary basis from various battlefield Waffen-SS formations, and who continued to sport their unit insignia. The Unterscharführer on the left, however, wears the double-armed swastika collar patch of a permanent non-SS camp guard.* IWM

Plate 107: *A concentration camp guard, February 1945. This is one of only three known photographs showing the double-armed swastika collar patch being worn. It was used from September 1944 to identify full-time concentration camp guards who had been compulsorily transferred in from the Wehrmacht, SA, Werkschutz or similar non-SS organisations. Note also the two-part cap insignia and the dark green tunic collar, still being worn at this late stage in the war.*

106

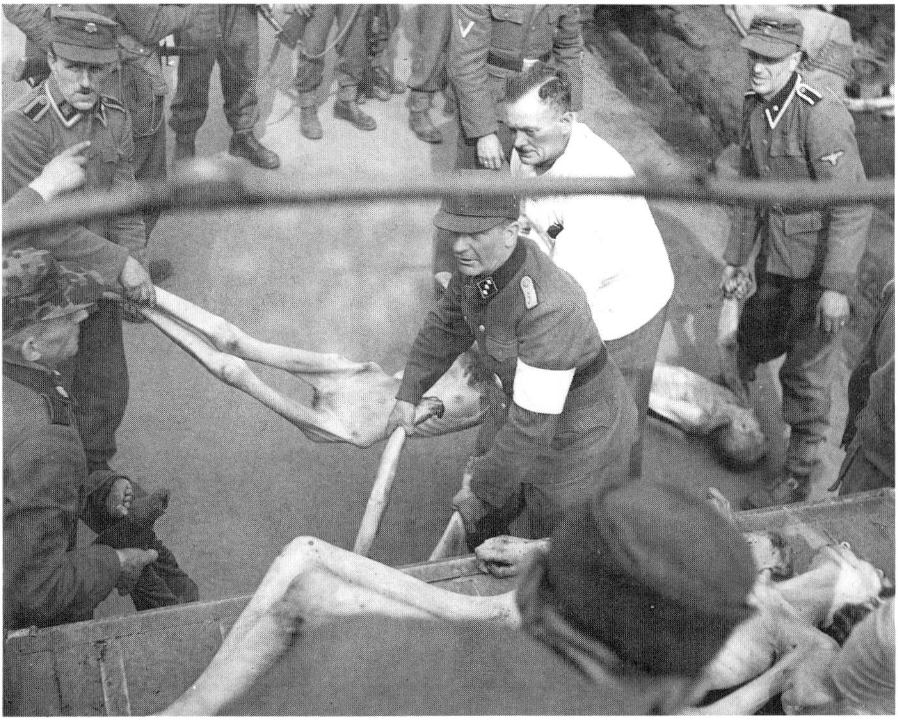

these patches unbordered for the rest of the war.

With the increasing recruitment of non-Germans into the Waffen-SS after 1940, Himmler became concerned about the use of the SS runes insignia by those not racially suitable for full SS membership, and he instructed that such recruits should wear some other form of badge on the right collar patch. The SS thereafter designed and issued a range of appropriate (and sometimes inappropriate!) collar patches for its foreign units and, pending the distribution of these insignia, blank patches were often worn in new units as an interim measure. German SS officers and NCOs serving in foreign formations were still entitled to wear the SS runes collar patch and, as from July 1943, if they chose to identify with their men by wearing the distinctive unit patch, they were obliged to sport the SS runes embroidered below the left breast pocket instead. The latter insignia was identical to that worn by SS men in the German police.

The wearing of collar patches did not always conform to regulations. Matching patches and vertical death's heads, although prohibited in 1940, continued to be worn well into 1942, and officers often used other ranks' patches in the field, or removed the cording from their own patches. In 1943, machine-woven versions of the SS runes and horizontal death's head patches were produced, but the earlier embroidered examples were still being issued at the end of the war. Recruits under training often wore no collar patches at all.

The following table lists all SS-VT, SS-TV and Waffen-SS unit collar patches which have been confirmed by contemporary photographic or documentary evidence. They were produced in embroidered versions only, unless otherwise indicated.

Design	***Period Used***	***Unit/Worn by***
Blank	1933-45	Specialists/Departmental or HQ Staff/Units not yet allocated patches
SS	1933-45	LAH, then from 1940 all German and Germanic units not allocated other patches
SS/large 1	1934	SS PB 'Süd'
SS/large 2	1934	SS PB 'Südwest'

Design	*Period Used*	*Unit/Worn by*
SS/large 3	1934	SS PB 'Mitte'
D	1934-37	Dachau Guard Battalion
K	1934-37	Concentration Camp Staff
Ü	1934-37	Dachau Training Camp
SS/T	1934-40	Bad Tölz Officers' School
SS/pick & shovel	1934-40	SS-VT Pioneer Battalion
SS/lightning bolt	1934-40	SS-VT Signals Battalion
SS/small 1	1935-40	'Deutschland'
SS/B	1935-40	Braunschweig Officers' School
SS/V	1935-40	Administration School
Vertical death's head	1936-42	Totenkopf Units
Vertical death's head/I-V	1936-37	SS-TV Battalion Staff
Vertical death's head/1-26	1936-40	SS-TV Companies
Vertical death's head/S	1936-40	SS-TV Medical Battalion
SS/small 2	1936-40	'Germania'
SS/S	1936-40	SS-VT Medical Battalion
SS/N	1936-40	'Nürnberg'
Vertical death's head/K	1937-40	Concentration Camp Staff
SS/small 3	1938-40	'Der Führer'
Police litzen	1939-42	Police-Division
Police litzen (woven)	1939-42	Police-Division
Horizontal death's head	1940-45	Totenkopf Units
Lion with axe	1941-43	Norwegian Legion
Lion with axe (metal)	1941-43	Norwegian Legion
Wolfsangel	1941-45	Dutch Legion/'Nederland'
Trifos	1941-45	'Nordwest'/Freikorps Danmark/ Flemish Legion/'Langemarck'
Lyre	1941-45	Music School
Danish Flag	1942	Freikorps Danmark
Odal-Rune	1942-45	'Prinz Eugen'
Open sonnenrad	1943-45	'Nordland'
SS (woven)	1943-45	All German and Germanic Units not allocated other patches
Horizontal death's head (woven)	1943-45	Totenkopf Units
Scimitar & swastika	1943-45	'Handschar'
Lion rampant	1943-45	14th Division
Swastika	1943-45	Latvian Legion/15th Division/ 19th Division
Sun & stars	1944-45	15th Division
E & mailed arm/sword	1944-45	20th Division
Cornflower	1944-45	'Maria Theresa'
H	1944-45	'Hunyadi'
Crossed rifles & grenade	1944-45	Dirlewanger Brigade/36th Division
Three lions passant	1944-45	British Free Corps
Double-armed swastika	1944-45	Non-SS Concentration Camp Guards
Flaming grenade	1945	'Landstorm Nederland'
Flaming grenade (metal)	1945	'Landstorm Nederland'

A large number of other embroidered collar patches exist which cannot be authenticated by contemporary photographic or documentary evidence. Some of these are said to have been found at the SS-Bekleidungslager at Dachau in April 1945, but until proof of their existence prior to that date is uncovered there must be grave doubts as to their originality. Most, if not all, are probably postwar fabrications, based on prototype drawings and descriptions or spurious illustrations in modern books. The following table lists these 'alleged' SS collar patches.

Design	***Year Allegedly Produced***	***Unit/Intended for Wear by***
SS/flaming grenade	Unknown	Probably Ordnance Related
SS/crossed lances	Unknown	Mounted Units
Viking longship	1941	Norwegian Legion/'Wiking'
Closed sonnenrad	1943	Danes in 'Nordland'
W	1944	Non-SS Concentration Camp Guards
Trident of Vladimir	1944	14th Division/30th Division
SA rune	1944	'Horst Wessel'
Goat's head helmet	1944	'Skanderbeg'
Sunburst	1944	'Kama'
Karst flower	1944	24th Division
Cross of St George	1944	29th Division (Russian)
Fasces	1944	29th Division (Italian)
Sword & wreath	1944	29th Division (Italian)
SS (on red patch)	1944	29th Division (Italian)
Cross of Burgundy	1945	'Wallonien'
Russian Orthodox Cross	1945	30th Division
Closed sonnenrad	1945	33rd Division (Hungarian)
Sword of St Joan	1945	'Charlemagne'
Crossed grenades	1945	36th Division
Wolf's head	1945	Crimean Tartars
Sword & shield	1945	Caucasians
Tiger's head	1945	Indian Legion

108

Plate 108: *Sig-runes insignia worn below the left breast pocket from July 1943 to identify SS members serving in foreign Waffen-SS formations with their own distinctive non-runic collar patches.*

Members of the Armed SS wore standard Allgemeine-SS shoulder straps on the right side only until 1935, when the earth-grey uniform was introduced. In July of that year, SS-VT officers were ordered to wear their Allgemeine-SS straps on both shoulders of the grey uniform. Other ranks received army-pattern straps made of plain earth-grey material, or earth-brown for SS-TV troops. In 1936, these enlisted men's shoulder straps were replaced first by a round-ended black version piped in black/aluminium twisted cord, then by an unpiped black type with pointed ends. None of these early straps identified the wearer's rank, as that was shown by his collar patches.

In March 1938, army-pattern straps with black underlay and gilt stars were issued to all Armed SS officers, and NCOs began to wear aluminium lace, or tresse, and white metal 'pips'. Rank was thereafter clearly indicated by the straps. From December 1939, officers sported coloured Waffenfarbe piping between the aluminium braid and black underlay, and other ranks received their definitive Waffenfarbe-piped black straps with rounded ends.

A large number of unit identification insignia were worn on the shoulder straps. For officers, these numerals and cyphers were initially in gilt metal, then bronze after 1940. Other ranks had them embroidered directly onto their straps, or onto

109

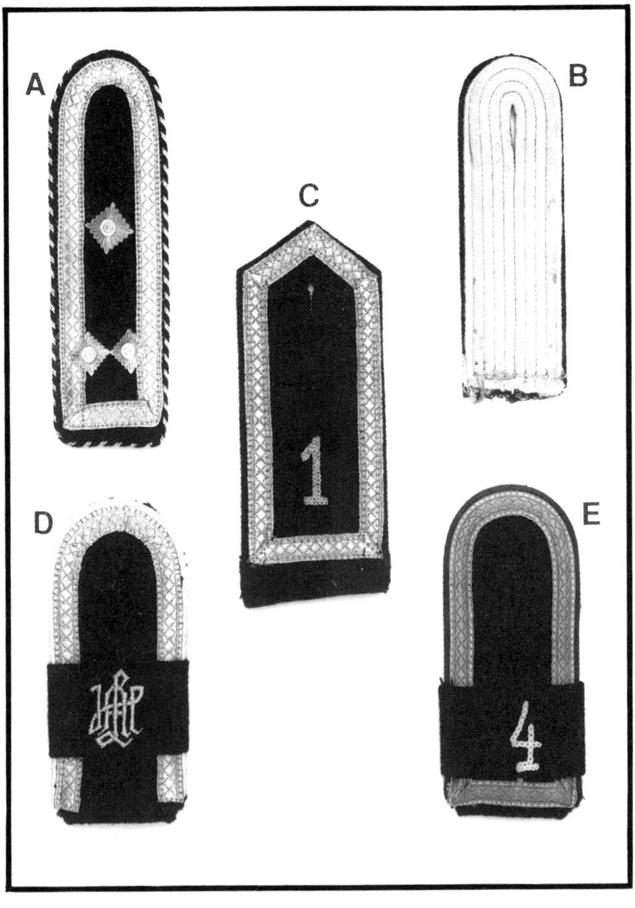

Plate 109: *A selection of Waffen-SS shoulder straps. These are:*

- *A M38 strap with obsolete black/aluminium twisted cord piping, for an SS-VT Sturmscharführer.*
- *B M39 strap with white Waffenfarbe piping, for an SS-Untersturmführer.*
- *C M38 strap with chain stitch '1', for a Scharführer in SS-Totenkopfstandarte 1 'Oberbayern'.*
- *D M40 strap with white Waffenfarbe piping and machine-embroidered 'LAH' slip-on tab for an Unterscharführer in the Leibstandarte.*
- *E M40 strap with chain stitch '4' slip-on tab, for a Scharführer in the 4th SS-Totenkopf Infantry Regiment.*

Plate 110: *Underside of a typical other ranks' shoulder strap, showing the field-grey woollen reinforcement on the reverse of the upper portion and the cotton twill backing to the retaining tab.*

110

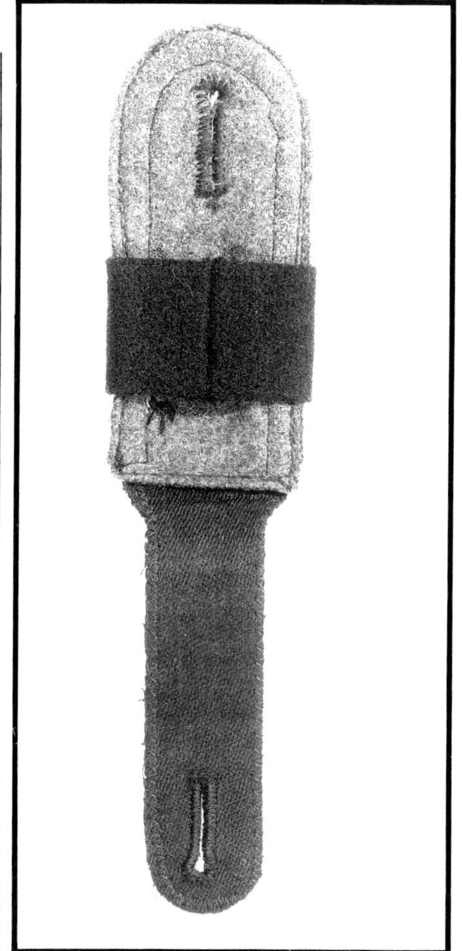

removable slip-on tabs from 1940. The following table lists the various identification badges known to have been used on Waffen-SS shoulder straps.

Badge	*Unit*
A	SS-VT Artillery Regiment
A (Gothic)	SS-VT Reconnaissance Battalion
AS/I	Artillery School I
AS/II	Artillery School II
Cogwheel	Technical Units
D	'Deutschland' Standarte
DF	'Der Führer' Standarte
E/Roman Numeral	Recruiting Offices
Fl	SS-VT Anti-Aircraft MG Battalion
G	'Germania' Standarte
JS/B	Junkerschule Braunschweig
JS/T	Junkerschule Tölz
L	Motor Technical School
L (Gothic)	Training Establishments
LAH	Leibstandarte-SS 'Adolf Hitler'
Lyre	Bands
MS	Musikschule Braunschweig
N	'Nordland' Standarte
P (Gothic)	SS-VT Anti-Tank Battalion
Serpent	Veterinary Units
Serpent & Staff	Medical Units
SK/D	Dachau Garrison
SK/P	Prague Garrison
US/L	Unterführerschule Lauenburg
US/R	Unterführerschule Radolfzell
W	'Westland' Standarte
1-17	Totenkopf Standarten0.5

In October 1943, Himmler decided that Waffen-SS units and specialist personnel were adequately identified by collar patches, cuff titles and sleeve diamonds, and he forbade the wearing of shoulder strap numerals and cyphers for the duration of the war. The only exception was the Leibstandarte-SS 'Adolf Hitler', whose members were permitted to retain their LAH monograms.

111

Plate 111: *SS-Gruppenführer Walter Krüger, commander of 'Das Reich' in September 1943. He wears the heavily embroidered shoulder straps of a Waffen-SS General.*

112

The cuff title, a woven black tape about 28mm in width and 49cm in length which was worn on the lower left sleeve of the tunic and greatcoat, became one of the most distinctive features of SS uniform. Apart from identifying the unit of the wearer, it was partly responsible for the remarkable *esprit de corps* of the Waffen-SS.

All prewar regiments and most ancillary formations of the SS-VT and SS-TV had their own cuff titles, which were handed over as part and parcel of the clothing issue. Each man received four, one for each of his uniforms, and they were expected to last him nine months. These early cuff titles were embroidered in Gothic lettering with the exception of the Leibstandarte's 'Adolf Hitler' insignia, which featured the hand-written Sütterlin script officially reserved for the Führer's guards from 1936.

On 1 September 1939, the Gothic 'SS' used on certain cuff titles was replaced by a runic version, and three months later all Gothic script was discontinued in favour of standard Latin lettering.

In May 1940, the cuff titles worn by ancillary Waffen-SS units, for example 'SS-Nachrichtensturmbann' and 'SS-Pioniersturmbann', were abolished as it was felt that they constituted a security risk. Regimental titles such as 'Deutschland' continued to be used, however, even after the introduction of divisional titles. The latter did not materialise until 1942 and were worn by divisional personnel not entitled to regimental cuff titles. So a member of the signals battalion in the SS-Verfügungsdivision would wear the 'SS-Nachrichtensturmbann' title until May 1940, then no cuff title at all, and finally the 'Das Reich' title as from September 1942.

As the war progressed, cuff titles took on a new significance and were presented at solemn ceremonies during which unit

Plate 112: *An Untersturmführer of an SS-V ancillary unit, denoted by his lack of regimental cuff title, during a lull in the western Blitzkrieg, May 1940.*

commanders would remind recipients of the great honour being bestowed upon then and that they should do nothing to disgrace the names which their cuff titles bore. The exact criteria for awarding names and cuff titles is not known, but what is certain is that many SS divisions, like the 14th and 15th, were never named, while some of those which were, such as 'Handschar' and 'Maria Theresa', never received cuff titles. Himmler apparently judged every application on its own merits, refusing some new units on the grounds that a cuff title had to be earned on the field of battle, and turning down others because they had been formed as a temporary wartime expedient from personnel considered racially unsuitable for SS membership.

Any Waffen-SS soldier transferring from one unit to another had to remove his old cuff title and replace it with that of his new unit. However, if the latter had not been awarded a cuff title, the man was permitted to continue to wear the title of his former unit. That explains why 'Adolf Hitler' and 'Der Führer' cuff titles featured amongst the officer cadre of the 24th SS Division in northern Italy at the end of the war, and why miscellaneous cuff titles were worn by SS paratroopers.

On occasion two cuff titles could be worn together. Officer cadets being trained at Bad Tölz, for example, were initially allowed to wear the 'SS-Schule Tölz' cuff title above their own regimental or divisional titles, while war correspondents and military policemen often wore the 'SS-Kriegsberichter' and 'SS-Feldgendarmerie' titles below those of the regiment or division to which they were attached. The wearing of more than one cuff title in this fashion was forbidden in August 1943.

Cuff titles fell into the following four categories according to the method of their manufacture:

(i) ***Hand-embroidered in aluminium wire or thread***

Produced from 1933 until June 1942. For wear by all ranks until 1936, and thereafter by officers only.

(ii) ***Machine-embroidered in white or silver-grey cotton thread***

The so-called 'RZM-style'. Produced from 1936-43 for wear by other ranks only.

Plate 113: *The Leibstandarte's 'Adolf Hitler' cuff title, hand-embroidered in Sütterlin script. This photograph of a captured tunic was taken by a British War Correspondent in 1945. The Crimea Shield has been placed for effect only, and would normally be sewn on to the upper sleeve.* IWM

(iii) ***Machine-woven in aluminium thread***

Produced from 1939-43 for wear by officers only.

(iv) ***Machine-woven in flat grey cotton or silken thread***

The so-called 'BEVO' pattern. Produced from 1943-45 for wear by all ranks.

While the foregoing details the intended recipients of the various manufacturing styles, it was not uncommon for officers to use other ranks' cuff titles on their field tunics, or for NCOs to acquire officer quality titles, for wear on their dress uniforms. Moreover, old stocks of some early cuff titles continued to be worn long after they had been officially discontinued.

These categories are most important from a collector's point of view, for some cuff titles which appear on the market can readily be identified as reproductions simply because the date of introduction of the original does not correspond with the manufacturing technique of the copy. Cuff titles such as 'Florian Geyer', 'Hohenstaufen' and 'Reichsführer-SS', for example, which dated from 1943 and later, were all made in the BEVO pattern and should not be encountered in the earlier RZM-style. Similarly, Gothic script had been abandoned long before 1943 so it follows that Gothic lettering should not feature on BEVO cuff titles.

The table below lists all SS-VT, SS-TV and Waffen-SS cuff titles which have been confirmed by contemporary photographic or documentary evidence, together with their known manufacturing styles.

KEY		
	HE	Hand-embroidered in aluminium wire or thread
	RZM	Machine-embroidered in white or silver-grey cotton thread
	MW	Machine-woven in aluminium thread
	BEVO	Machine-woven in flat grey cotton or silken thread

Title	***Year Introduced***	***Manufacturing Style***
Adolf Hitler	1933	HE, RZM, MW, BEVO
Brandenburg	1937	HE, RZM
British Free Corps	1944	Manufacturing style cannot be discerned from the few surviving wartime photographs of members of this tiny unit. Probably hand-embroidered as only a very small quantity was required
Danmark	1943	BEVO
Das Reich	1942	RZM, MW, BEVO
Death's Head (insignia)	1938	HE, MW
Den Norske Legion	1941	HE
Der Führer	1938	HE, RZM, MW, BEVO
De Ruiter	1943	BEVO
Deutschland	1935	HE, RZM, MW
Elbe	1937	HE, RZM
E SS/TV	1939	MW
Florian Geyer	1944	BEVO
Freikorps Danmark	1941	RZM
Frundsberg	1943	BEVO
Frw. Legion Flandern	1941	RZM
Frw. Legion Nederland	1941	RZM
Frw. Legion Niederlande	1941	RZM, MW
Frw. Legion Norwegen	1941	RZM
General Seyffardt	1943	BEVO
Germania	1936	HE, RZM, MW, BEVO
Götz von Berlichingen	1943	BEVO

Title	Year Introduced	Manufacturing Style
Hermann von Salza	1944	BEVO
Hitlerjugend	1943	BEVO
Hohenstaufen	1943	BEVO
Horst Wessel	1944	BEVO
Kdtr. Ü.L. Dachau	1935	HE
Kurt Eggers	1943	RZM, BEVO
Langemarck	1942	RZM, MW
Legion Niederlande	1941	HE
Legion Norwegen	1941	RZM
Michael Gaissmair	1944	BEVO
Nederland	1944	BEVO
Nordland	1940	HE, RZM, MW, BEVO
Nordwest	1941	RZM
Norge	1943	BEVO
Oberbayern	1937	HE, RZM, MW
Ostfriesland	1937	HE, RZM
Ostmark	1938	MW
Police Eagle (insignia)	1942	MW
Prinz Eugen	1942	RZM, MW, BEVO
Reichsführer-SS	1943	BEVO
Reichsführung-SS	1940	HE

114

115

Plate 114: *Two regulation Waffen-SS cuff titles. 'Westland' is in the RZM-style, machine-embroidered in raised silver-grey cotton with seven-strand aluminium borders. 'Götz von Berlichingen' is of the BEVO pattern, machine-woven in flat grey cotton on a silken base.*

Plate 115: *Reverse of a BEVO-woven 'Reichsführer-SS' cuff title , showing the typical black-and-white chequered effect with loose threads behind the wording.*

Title	*Year Introduced*	*Manufacturing Style*
Reichsschule-SS	1943	BEVO
Reinhard Heydrich	1942	RZM, MW, BEVO
Sachsen	1937	HE, RZM
Sanitätsabteilung	1936	HE, RZM
Skanderbeg	1944	BEVO
SS-Ärtzliche Akademie	1939	MW
SS-Feldgendarmerie	1942	MW, BEVO
SS-Heimwehr Danzig	1939	RZM
SS-Inspektion	1936	HE
SS-KB-Abt	1941	RZM
SS-Kriegsberichter	1940	HE, RZM, BEVO
SS-Kriegsberichter-Kp	1940	Unofficial Sütterlin script in chain stitch embroidery
SS-Musikschule Braunschweig	1941	RZM
SS-Nachrichtensturmbann	1937	HE, RZM
SS-Pioniersturmbann	1937	HE, RZM
SS-Polizei-Division	1942	RZM, MW, BEVO
SS-Schule Braunschweig	1935	HE (Sütterlin until 1936), RZM
SS-Schule Tölz	1934	HE, RZM
SS-Totenkopfverbände	1937	MW
SS-Übungslager Dachau	1937	HE, RZM
SS-Unterführerschule	1940	HE, RZM
SS-Verwaltungsschule	1935	HE
Theodor Eicke	1943	BEVO
Thule	1942	RZM, MW
Thüringen	1937	HE, MW
Totenkopf	1942	RZM, MW, BEVO
Wallonien	1944	BEVO
W.B. Dachau	1935	HE
Westland	1940	HE, RZM, MW, BEVO
Wiking	1942	RZM, MW, BEVO

A few rare variant cuff titles are also known to have existed, but these were unofficial and even unique in some cases. Examples include Sepp Dietrich's wartime 'Adolf Hitler' cuff titles, which were hand-embroidered in gold bullion, and the 'Wiking' and 'Wallonien' cuff titles hand-embroidered in Gothic script for wear by Herbert Gille and Léon Degrelle respectively. A small number of unapproved localised cuff titles, such as the 'Narwa' and 'Estland' titles worn by some members of the 20th SS Division, are confirmed from photographs and were in all probability hand-embroidered. These are the exceptions which prove the general rules of cuff title manufacture.

The following cuff titles were authorised during the war, but never issued for a variety of reasons:

Artur Phleps
Charlemagne
Finnisches Frw. Bataillon der Waffen-SS
Hinrich Schuldt
30 Januar
Landstorm Nederland
Latvija
Osttürkischer Waffen-Verband der SS
Woldemars Veiss

Most of these cuff titles existed on paper only. Examples of the 'Charlemagne' 'Landstorm Nederland' and 'Osttürkischer Waffen-Verband der SS' titles have appeared in a manufactured form, but these have yet to be authenticated by photographic or documentary evidence.

The eagle and swastika was established as the national emblem, or Hoheitsabzeichen, of the Third Reich on 7 March 1936. The insignia was ultimately developed to incorporate a wide variety of forms, but the eagle invariably faced to its right when being used by State organisations such as the Police and Customs Service, and to its left when being worn by the NSDAP and Party organisations like the SA and NSKK.

The first SS tunic eagles were sported by Sepp Dietrich and others as early as the summer of 1935, with the newly-introduced earth-grey uniform. The use of eagles on the right breast was restricted by law to the army, navy and air force, so members of the LAH and SS-VT took to wearing theirs on the upper left arm, in lieu of the gaudy Allgemeine-SS armband which was clearly unsuitable for field use. The pattern of sleeve eagle officially adopted by the Armed SS in May 1936 was that introduced simultaneously for the Railway Police, with a right-facing eagle having dipping wings. It was discontinued after only two years, but was still being worn by some SS veterans as late as 1943.

The second and definitive pattern of SS national emblem, with a left-facing eagle and straight wings tapering to a point, was devised in 1938 and was eventually produced in several variations to become one of the most distinctive features of Waffen-SS uniform. The commonest manufacturing method was machine-embroidery, in white or silver-grey cotton thread on black, and these RZM-style eagles came in the following three types, dependent upon period of production:

Type 1 with a pronounced square head (1938-41)

Type 2 with a less pronounced curved head (1942-43)

Type 3 with a shallow round head (1944-45)

Photographs confirm these types time and time again as period, rather than manufacturers', variations. The square-headed 'Type 1' eagle can regularly be seen in pre-war shots and pictures taken during the western and Balkan Blitzkriegs of 1940-41, while the round-headed insignia never features in these photographs. Conversely, the round-headed 'Type 3' eagle is consistently seen being worn on camouflage drill tunics during the Normandy and Ardennes battles, with the 'Type 1' badge being conspicuous by its absence at that stage of the war.

In 1939, a BEVO machine-woven version of the 1938-pattern SS sleeve eagle began to appear, in flat grey cotton or silken thread for other ranks and fine silver wire for officers. It was widely worn on all types of Waffen-SS uniform throughout the war and was even used as a cap badge by female SS auxiliaries. The BEVO eagle was also produced in tan-brown from 1943, for the tropical uniform. A few examples in green weave, allegedly for use on the spring side of the camouflage uniform, have made their way on to the market recently, but their authenticity is very much in doubt.

116

Plate 116: *An Obersturmführer of the SS-TV Medical Battalion, temporarily seconded to the army for training purposes in 1939. In addition to the standard SS sleeve eagle, he wears the army eagle above his right breast pocket. This is the only known photograph showing both of these insignia being worn simultaneously.*

117

118

Plate 117: *The BEVO machine-woven version of the SS arm eagle for other ranks.*

Plate 118: *Machine-embroidered SS arm eagle with a shallow round head, as worn during the 1944-45 period.*

The SS arm eagle was also hand-embroidered in silver bullion for officers. Numerous varieties existed, some with distinctly formed swastikas and others with swastikas which filled the entire wreath. A few had snaps attached to the rear so that they could readily be removed from the tunic when the latter was being cleaned. The bullion eagle was standard wear for all SS officers, although Sepp Dietrich again highlighted his unique status by having his insignia executed in gold wire.

In addition to the various regulation types of the 1938-pattern SS Hoheitsabzeichen, other eagles were sometimes worn on the left arm of the Waffen-SS tunic. A number of ex-army officers who transferred to the Waffen-SS, and foreigners who had previously served in Wehrmacht legions, wore the army breast eagle on the sleeve, either to emphasise their origins or simply because the army eagle was more readily available to them. The use of army eagles was particularly common during the rapid expansion of the Waffen-SS in 1939-40, when SS eagles were in short supply and army-style Waffenfarbe piping and matching collar patches were the order of the day. A few SS-VT and SS-TV men on secondment to army units even wore the army eagle on the right breast while still sporting the SS eagle on the left arm! The Italian SS had their own version of the sleeve eagle, which was right-facing and clutched a fasces instead of a swastika, and between August 1942 and October 1944 the German Police eagle in orange thread was worn by members of the SS-Feldgendarmerie.

Plate 119 : *Sepp Dietrich had a unique arm eagle hand-embroidered in gold bullion.*

119

The following insignia were authorised for use on LAH, SS-VT, SS-TV and Waffen-SS cloth headgear:

(i) The Prussian-pattern death's head in metal, for wear on the peaked cap and krätzchen (1933-34)
(ii) The 1929-pattern NSDAP eagle in metal, for the peaked cap and krätzchen (1933-36)
(iii) The 1929-pattern NSDAP eagle in machine-embroidery, for the Model 1934 schiffchen field cap (1934-36)
(iv) The 1934-pattern death's head in metal, for the peaked cap and NCO's 1938 field cap (1934-45)
(v) The 1934-pattern death's head button in metal, for the M34 schiffchen field cap (1934-40)
(vi) The 1936-pattern SS eagle in metal, for the peaked cap and NCO's M38 field cap (1936-45)
(vii) The 1936-pattern SS eagle in machine-embroidery, for the M34 schiffchen field cap (1936-40)
(viii) The 1936-pattern SS eagle in machine-embroidery for the Panzer beret (1938-40)
(ix) The variant death's head in machine-embroidery for the Panzer beret (1938-40)
(x) The 1934-pattern death's head in BEVO weave for the Model 1940 schiffchen, the Bergmütze, the Einheitsfeldmütze and the fez (1940-45)
(xi) The 1936-pattern SS eagle in BEVO weave for the M40 schiffchen, the Bergmütze, the Einheitsfeldmütze and the fez (1940-45)
(xii) BEVO eagles and death's heads in green and brown for the camouflage field cap (1942)
(xiii) BEVO eagles and death's heads in tan-brown for the tropical field cap (1943-45)

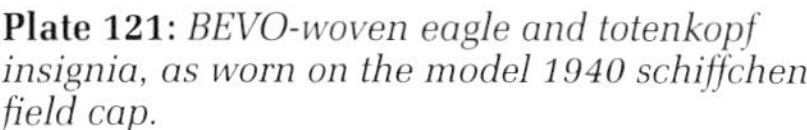

Plate 121: *BEVO-woven eagle and totenkopf insignia, as worn on the model 1940 schiffchen field cap.*

120

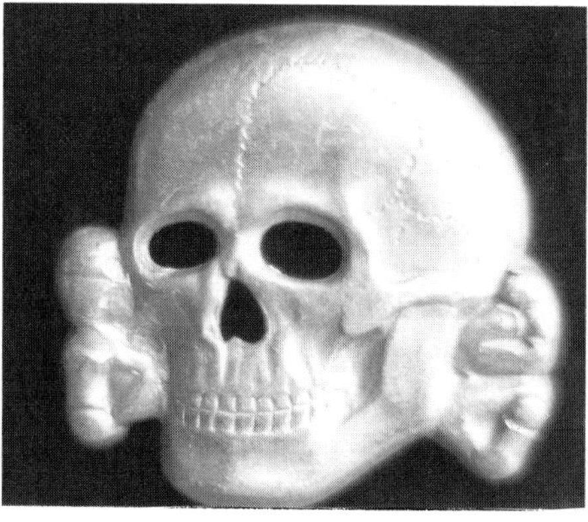

Plate 120: *1934-pattern death's head in copper-plated aluminium with a silver surface wash. This example is marked 'RZM 499/41' and has two round steel prongs on the reverse. Note the fine detailing and angular jawline characteristic of originals.*

(xiv) One-piece machine-embroidered or BEVO-woven eagle/death's head insignia on a triangular background, for the Einheitsfeldmütze (1943-45)
(xv) The variant SS eagle in metal clutching a fasces, for the Italian SS peaked cap (1944-45)

(Many of these badges, particularly nos (iii), (viii), (ix), (xii), (xiii), (xiv) and (xv), were seldom issued and are now exceptionally rare.)

121

122

While the above badges were prescribed by regulations, they were often interchanged between headgear. For example, Prussian-pattern death's heads were worn late into the war by the Old Guard, metal schirmmütze insignia was frequently used on field caps, and woven badges occasionally appeared on peaked caps. Moreover, a huge variety of semi-official and unofficial alternative insignia were also adopted. These included:

(i) SS arm eagles – sewn on field caps and winter fur headdress;
(ii) Army eagles – widely worn in all their forms on all types of SS headgear;
(iii) NSDAP eagles – often seen on peaked caps;
(iv) Embroidered or woven death's heads removed from SS-TV collar patches used on field caps and winter headgear;
(v) Metal death's heads removed from army Panzer collar patches – pinned to schiffchen field caps.

Plate 122: *Standard SS runic shield decal for the steel helmet. The helmet in this case has clearly seen some considerable front-line service, and the decal was resilient enough to withstand it. Scores and marks on the paintwork can be seen to continue into the battered decal.*

Hand-embroidered SS cap eagles in silver bullion were not officially authorised, and such pieces which are offered today tend to be postwar productions.

The decals used on Waffen-SS steel helmets were more consistent in following the prescribed regulations for wear, since they were applied in the factory rather than in the field. The sole exception was the occasional use of the runic insignia on the left side of the helmet instead of (or in addition to) the right, possibly as an interim measure following the discontinuation of the swastika shield in 1940. It seems unlikely that the double runic decals were intended for some foreign formations, as has been suggested, since these were the very units which Himmler generally did not wish to see sporting the SS runes! Decals were applied using Ducolux, Kopal and Damar lacquers over a 24-hour period and were very resistant to wear, unlike modern copies which can easily be scraped off.

Members of the Polizei-Division wore Police headgear until the beginning of 1942 when the unit was fully incorporated into the Waffen-SS. Steel helmets were standard Police issue, but a range of peaked caps including Police, army and Waffen-SS types were utilised, all bearing Police badges. Field caps also varied, with the national cockade being discontinued in August 1941 in favour of a Waffenfarbe soutache. From 1942, the division adopted standard Waffen-SS uniforms and head-gear.

123

Plate 123: *Soldiers of the Polizei-Division using a mortar during training, April 1940. The man in the centre has been issued with a Waffen-SS steel helmet while the others wear Police helmets. Note also the mixture of Police collar patches with Waffen-SS shoulder straps, arm eagles and belt buckles.*

In addition to the foregoing insignia, which were common to most Waffen-SS personnel, a number of related badges existed which merit only brief coverage.

A range of arm shields was created for foreign volunteers in the Waffen-SS, and generally took the form of machine-embroidered national flags on a black cloth ground measuring around 60mm x 50mm. These were standardised in 1943, and most were produced by the Berlin firm of Tröltsch & Hanselmann. The shields were at first worn above the cuff title, and later beneath the SS arm eagle, and gradually replaced the army versions hitherto worn by many foreigners. The flags of Belgium, Denmark, Estonia, France, Great Britain, Holland, Latvia and Norway featured on these shields, while the badges for Albanian, Croatian, Finnish, Flemish and Ukrainian volunteers bore suitable heraldic motifs.

A series of trade badges to identify skills and specialities was designed in the shape of black cloth diamonds for wear on the lower left sleeve. Each badge was awarded after the successful completion of the relevant SS training course, and those who graduated from army schools were

Fig 18: *SS Trade Badges. These were worn on the left sleeve, above the cuff title, and denoted the following specialist appointments or qualifications:*

A	*Farrier*	*G*	*Medical orderly*
B	*Technical officer*	*H*	*Musician*
C	*Signaller*	*I*	*Legal officer*
D	*Transport NCO*	*J*	*Administrative officer*
E	*Veterinarian*	*K*	*Armourer NCO*
F	*Medical officer*	*L*	*Coxswain*

Plate 124: *A selection of foreign volunteer shields, many of which were Wehrmacht issue and continued to be worn when the units concerned were absorbed by the Waffen-SS during the last year of the war. Those shown identified:*

(a) Ukrainians
(b) Armenians
(c) Terek Cossacks
(d) Flemings
(e) Russians
(f) Croats
(g) Don Cossacks

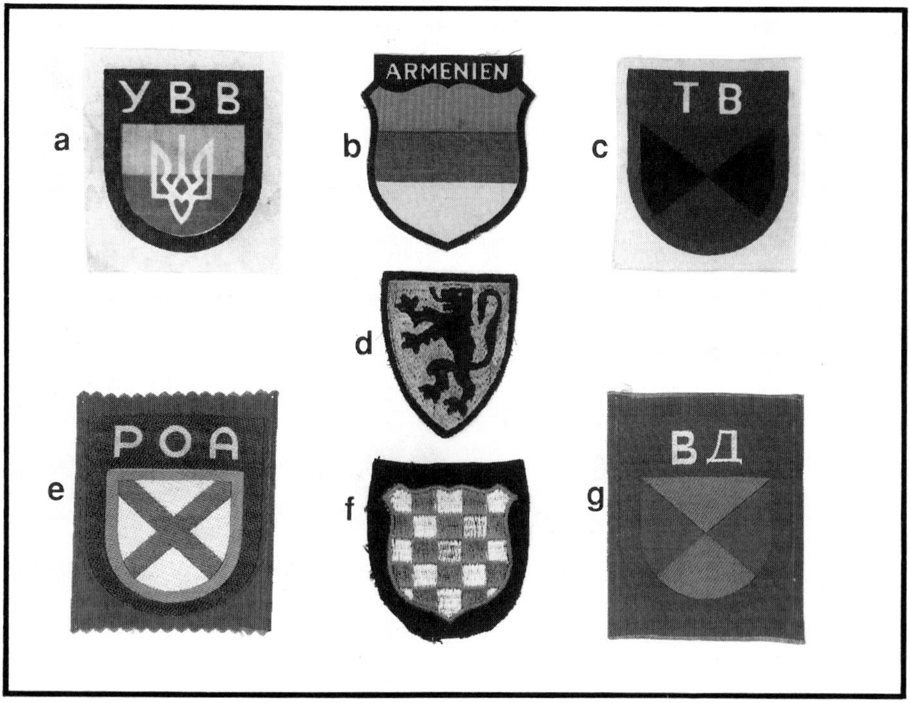

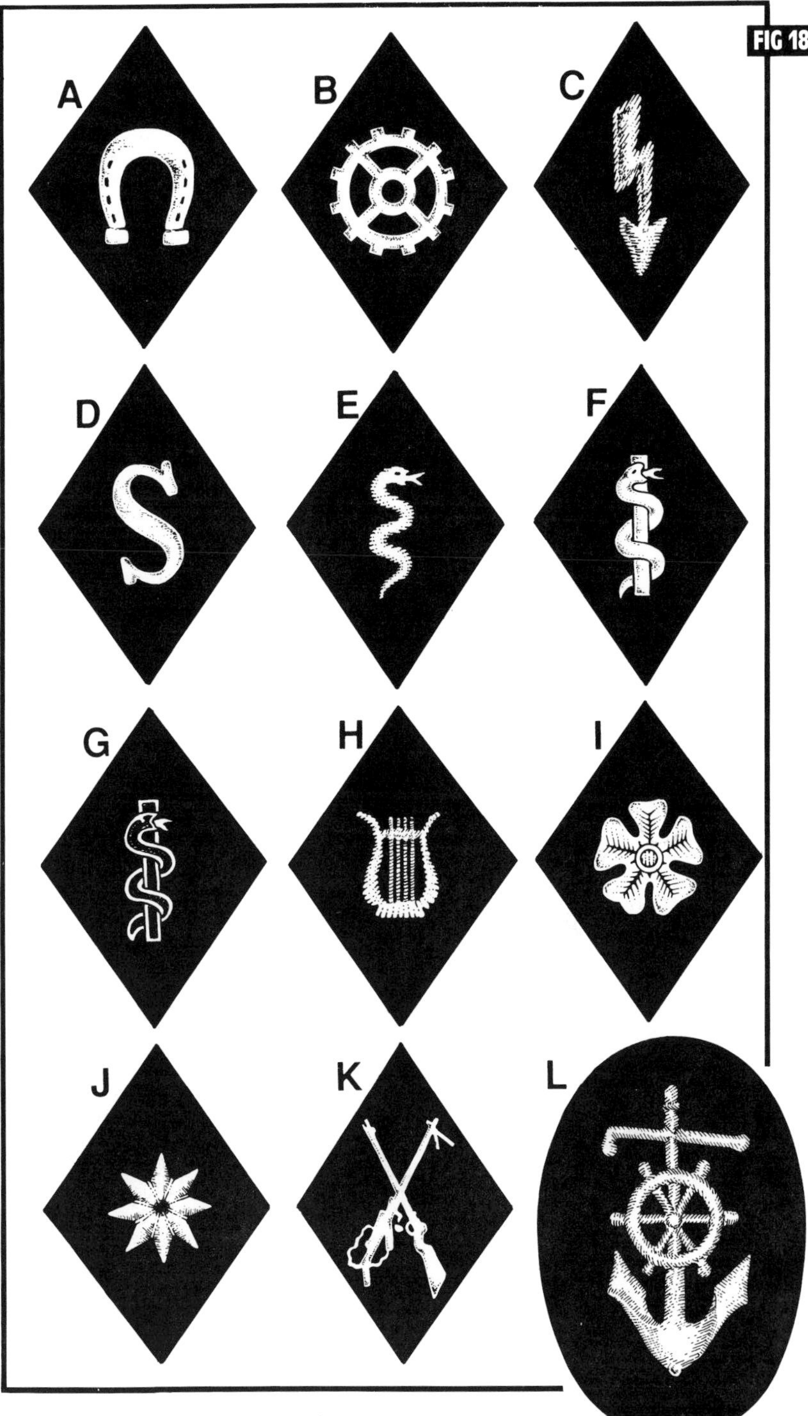
FIG 18
A
B
C
D
E
F
G
H
I
J
K
L

125

126

Plate 125: *Reverse views of the items shown in* **Plate 124**, *illustrating the varying characteristics of embroidered, woven and printed badges.*

Plate 126: *SS-Brigadeführer Karl Sauberzweig, commander of the 'Handschar' division, giving instructions to his driver in the spring of 1944. He wears the mountain troop edelweiss on his right sleeve. The Croat checkerboard shield of the division is also visible below the arm eagle of the officer standing at the driver's door.*

Fig 19: *The series of national armbands designed for young SS flak auxiliaries recruited from the occupied eastern territories. The runic triangle was worn by all members on the upper left sleeve.*

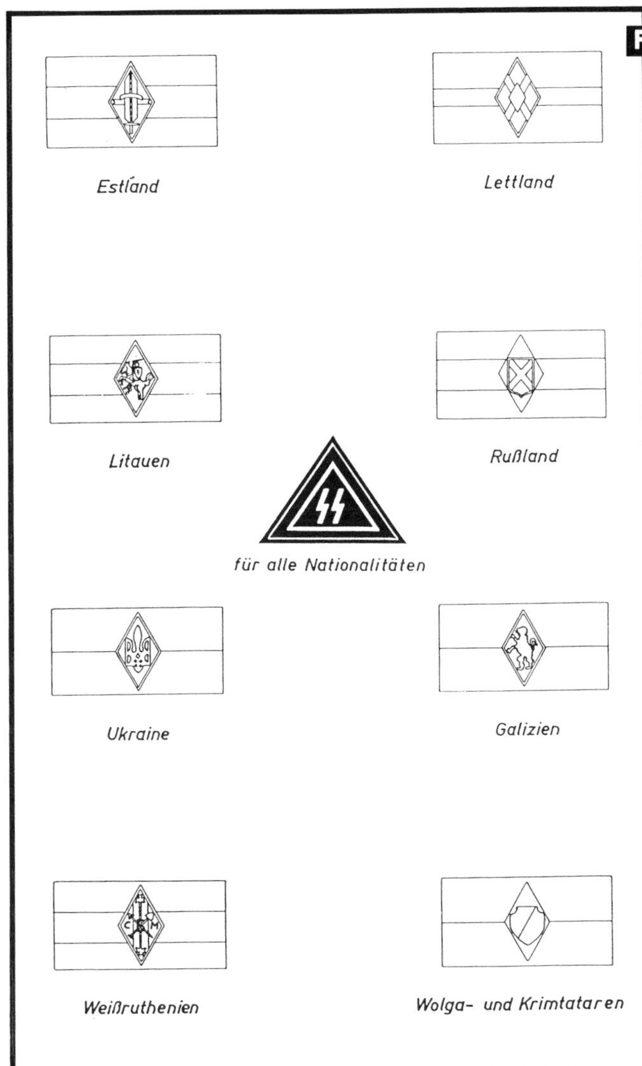

obliged to wear the army trade badge in lieu of the SS one. From October 1943, mountain troops sported a machine-embroidered edelweiss on the left side of the Bergmütze and on the right tunic sleeve, above the Honour Chevron of the Old Guard if the latter was also worn.

Uniformed female SS auxiliaries had a unique badge consisting of a black oval containing silver SS runes, which was sewn to the left breast pocket. Other civilian employees were given embroidered, woven or printed armbands bearing the wording 'Waffen-SS' or 'Im Dienste der Waffen-SS' when in the war zone, and brassards featuring national colours were worn by young SS flak helpers from the East. The latter were issued with a mixture of Luftwaffe and Hitler Youth uniform, and a printed triangular SS runes badge at the top of the left sleeve, in the manner of the HJ district triangle, was the only insignia which denoted their technical attachment to the Waffen-SS.

During World War 2, Waffen-SS soldiers were eligible for the whole range of Nazi military decorations, including the Iron Cross, German Cross, War Merit Cross and so on. Participation in the Crimea, Demjansk and Kurland battles earned the appropriate campaign distinctions for men of the Leibstandarte, SS-Totenkopf-Division and VI. Waffen-Armeekorps der SS, while troops of all units wore Infantry Assault, General Assault, Flak and Panzer Battle Badges, the Tank Destruction Award and the Close Combat Clasp. Only the Guerrilla Warfare Badge, however, was singled out as being of specific relevance to the activities of the Waffen-SS, and for that reason it merits some detailed coverage.

Hitler's invasion of the Soviet Union in June 1941 soon resulted in the Wehrmacht facing an entirely new type of enemy — professionally organised partisans who attacked in large groups capable of taking on and defeating German units of battalion or even regimental strength. As the war progressed, similar partisan bands appeared in Poland, the Balkans, Italy and, to a lesser extent, France. The harshness of German policies towards the civilian population in the conquered eastern territories contributed in part to the rapid growth of resistance during the second half of 1941, and this resistance was largely characterised by partisan warfare.

The vastness of the area behind the German lines and the terrain of forests, mountains and marshes lent themselves to guerrilla attacks. The partisan movement stemmed from the presence in German-occupied territory of whole Red Army units that had been cut off by the rapidity of the German advance. As early as July 1941 the Central Committee of the Communist Party called upon Soviet citizens to join these units and take up arms, and the following year the Soviet High Command took steps to co-ordinate guerrilla activity by establishing the Central Staff of the Partisan Movement. Liaison officers, wireless equipment, weapons and supplies were provided in ever increasing numbers and partisan operations were fully integrated into Red Army strategy. In addition to widespread attacks on German communications, partisans made specific efforts in support of Soviet offensives, notably at Kursk, and were able to ease the progress of conventional forces by securing bridges and key installations in the path of their advance. Such a role was markedly more effective than partisan attempts to engage German forces in open combat or to liberate or defend territory, for German units always tended to be better and more heavily equipped than the partisans.

From the outset, the struggle between German and partisan was one without mercy. No quarter was expected or given. Atrocities committed against captured German soldiers were met with a policy of extermination on the part of the occupying forces. On entering Taganrog, for example, the Leibstandarte found the mutilated remains of six of its men who had been killed and thrown down a well. During the next three days, the unit shot some 4,000 Soviet prisoners as a reprisal. Constant harassing of the civilian population and major offensives against guerrilla groups failed to curtail the resistance, however, and tied down large numbers of troops. Vast tracts of German-occupied territory soon became virtual no-go areas, allowing the Soviets to co-ordinate partisan sabotage activities.

It quickly became obvious that it would be impossible for the Wehrmacht alone to maintain order throughout Russia and eastern Europe. Consequently, during 1942, a large number of German civil policemen, the Ordnungspolizei or Orpo, supplemented by Allgemeine-SS conscripts, were transferred to 30 newly created independent Police Regiments comprising around 100 battalions, each of 500 men. They were organised and equipped on military lines and served as security troops in the occupied territories. These German formations were later designated 'SS-Police' Regiments and gained a reputation for extreme brutality.

In October 1942, Himmler was made responsible for all anti-partisan operations. In a speech given shortly afterwards, he stated that the new enemy did not deserve

Plate 127: *An SS anti-partisan patrol in Byelorussia, summer 1942. The Rottenführer in front is armed with an obsolete Vollmer Erma submachine-gun, a police weapon issued in limited numbers to a few rear echelon Waffen-SS units.*

127

the title 'partisans', which had patriotic connotations, as they were simply members of outlaw gangs or 'banden'. These gangster guerrillas were to be rooted out and executed without trial. Himmler appointed SS-Obergruppenführer Erich von dem Bach as his Chief of Counter-Guerrilla Forces, or Chef der Bandenkampfverbände. Von dem Bach was a pathological Slav-hater who had been born 'von dem Bach-Zelewski' and had dropped the 'Zelewski' from his name around 1939 because he felt it sounded 'too Polish'. He realised that the territories to be controlled, especially in Russia, were so vast that even the SS-Police needed additional support, and so various pro-German local militias and home guard units composed mainly of Balts, Cossacks and Ukrainians were raised and consolidated into an auxiliary police force known as the Schutzmannschaft der Ordnungspolizei, or Schuma. Members were generally nationalists at heart whose main aim was the defeat of Communism, and they viewed the German forces as liberators.

In Poland, 12 SS-Police Regiments supported the Wehrmacht in maintaining order, backed up by the Polish police and 12 Schuma battalions. Fourteen SS-Police Regiments served in Byelorussia, as did seven Police Rifle Regiments which were mixed German-Russian units, and a vast number of Schuma battalions. In Estonia, 26 Schuma battalions were formed, and an estimated 15,000 Latvians and 13,000 Lithuanians served in 64 other Schuma battalions deployed right across the Eastern Front. The Ukraine alone supplied 70,000 volunteers to staff a further 71 Schuma bat-

128

Plate 128: *While he was HSSPf in Serbia, SS-Gruppenführer August Meyszner (left) was responsible for all counter-guerrilla operations in the country. Here he confers with SS-Obergruppenführer Arthur Phleps of the 'Prinz Eugen' division during the spring of 1943. Note the puttees worn by both men.*

talions. Tito's partisan movement in the Balkans was so strong that several entire Waffen-SS divisions, notably 'Prinz Eugen' and 'Handschar', were raised to combat it, and they were backed up by Croatian, Serbian and Albanian police units.

The largest German anti-partisan sweep of the war, Operation 'Cottbus', which took place in Byelorussia in June 1943, involved nearly 17,000 German troops and was conducted so brutally and ruthlessly that nothing, human or animal, was left alive in the zone of operations. Nevertheless, 'Cottbus' failed to trap its quarry and was a major setback for von dem Bach.

The partisans went from strength to strength and by the middle of 1944 numbered around 400,000 in Warsaw, 390,000 in Yugoslavia, 230,000 in the Baltic States, 150,000 in Byelorussia, 50,000 in northern Italy, 40,000 in the Ukraine, 40,000 in Greece and 35,000 in Albania. There were also hundreds of smaller local resistance groups in France, Holland, Belgium, Norway and Denmark. In August 1944 the partisan 'Polish Home Army' rose up in Warsaw, in anticipation of approaching Red Army assistance, but the latter never materialised. The rebels initially gained control of two-thirds of the city, but the ferocity of the SS and police response, which levelled Poland's capital, forced the guerrillas underground, into the sewers, where they were gradually reduced and defeated by forces equipped with armour and flamethrowers, supported by Luftwaffe Stuka squadrons. The crushing of the Warsaw Uprising was the greatest anti-partisan victory achieved by the Germans during the war. Von dem Bach, who personally commanded a Battle Group in Warsaw, received the Knight's Cross of the Iron Cross after the successful conclusion of the fighting.

The increasing ferocity of the war waged against the partisans eventually necessitated the creation of a new decoration to reward those who had been engaged upon it for a prolonged period. On 30 January 1944, Hitler instituted the Bandenkampfabzeichen, which translates literally as 'Bandit Battle Badge' but more accurately as 'Guerrilla Warfare Badge'. It is generally known by collectors as the 'Anti-Partisan War Badge', which was the translation adopted in early English language books on Third Reich decorations. Whilst it was open to members of all the German fighting services, and their foreign auxiliaries, the Guerrilla Warfare Badge was officially designated as a 'Kampfabzeichen der Waffen-SS und Polizei', or 'Waffen-SS and Police Battle Badge', and was the only War Badge so described during the Third Reich.

Award of the badge came under the auspices of Himmler and an order issued from his Field Headquarters on 1 February 1944 laid down the following:

1. The Guerrilla Warfare Badge is both a bravery and merit decoration.
2. It is awarded in three grades, Bronze, Silver and Gold.
3. The Guerrilla Warfare Badge can be awarded to all officers, NCOs and men engaged with the German forces in anti-Guerrilla operations.
4. The qualification for award is:
   - (a) Bronze — 20 combat days for ground troops; 30 combat days for Luftwaffe crews
   - (b) Silver — 50 combat days for ground troops; 75 combat days for Luftwaffe crews
   - (c) Gold — 100 combat days for ground troops; 150 combat days for Luftwaffe crews
5. For ground troops, a combat day is reckoned to be one during which they have taken part in close combat (man against man) with guerrillas. For Luftwaffe crews, a combat day is reckoned to be one during which they have exposed themselves to anti-aircraft fire from guerrilla forces. Being shot down counts as three combat days.
6. Combat days may be reckoned as from 1 January 1943.
7. The Guerrilla Warfare Badge may be worn on the left breast of all Wehrmacht, Police, SS and NSDAP uniforms.
8. The badge is awarded with a citation.
9. Posthumous presentations of awards in respect of those who have qualified for them prior to being killed in action will be made to their next-of-kin.

Plate 129: *The Guerrilla Warfare Badge in Bronze.*

Plate 130: *Reverse of the item illustrated in* **Plate 129**, *showing typical Juncker construction.*

Qualification for award was therefore very high, making the Bandenkampfabzeichen far more difficult to achieve than similar decorations like the Infantry Assault Badge.

Himmler reserved the right to award the Gold badge personally, which is hardly surprising since it was the equivalent of winning the Close Combat Clasp in Gold twice! The 'Völkischer Beobachter' of 21 February 1945 reported that 'The Reichsführer-SS yesterday presented the first Guerrilla Warfare Badges in Gold to four members of the Waffen-SS engaged in the fighting on the Adriatic Coast'. The first recipient was SS-Obersturmführer Erich Kühbandner of the 24th SS Division, which had been raised to combat partisans in the Carso and Julian Alps. While the badge was hard-won, however, Knight's Cross winner Hans Sturm, who was awarded the Bronze grade while serving with the Army in Italy, stated after the war that he never wore it as he did not wish to be associated with the atrocities which it represented. Several of his Wehrmacht counterparts appear to have been like-minded, for it is very seldom seen in wartime photographs. The Waffen-SS and Police, on the other hand, held the Guerrilla Warfare Badge in high regard and displayed it proudly on every possible occasion, giving it precedence over other War Badges. They saw it as 'their' badge, recognising their particular role in quelling rebellion behind the front-lines.

The design of the Guerrilla Warfare Badge was based on that of the insignia of the Silesian Freikorps of 1919 and featured a wreath of oakleaves enclosing a sword with sunwheel swastika (representing the German and auxiliary forces) plunging into a Hydra (the partisans). The badge has always been described in previous literature on the subject as featuring a nest of snakes, but that is not the case. Close examination confirms that the creature depicted is, in fact, a Hydra with a single tail and five heads. The Hydra was a fabulous multi-headed sea serpent of Greek mythology and was famed as being almost impossible to destroy since its heads grew quickly again if they were cut off. The parallel with the partisan forces, which sprang up vigorously time and time again, is obvious. At the sword's point was a totenkopf or death's head, which was doubly appropriate since it symbolised both the SS involvement and the deadly nature of the struggle which was being carried on.

129

All Guerrilla Warfare Badges were initially produced by the firm of C.E. Juncker, a prestigious medal and decoration manufacturing business sited at Alte Jakobstrasse 13, Berlin. It has been alleged, but not confirmed, that when the Juncker firm was bombed out towards the end of the war, production switched to another (unknown)

130

131

Plate 131: *Leibstandarte and 'Der Führer' officers attached to the 24th SS division surrender to the British near Treviso in northern Italy, 7 May 1945. The Obersturmführer on the left, with tropical field cap and shorts, wears the Guerrilla Warfare Badge in Silver above his other awards.* IWM

maker, resulting in two variants of the badge, the Juncker type with solid 'dots' on the sword handle and a second type with hollow 'dots'. It has also been suggested that Himmler ordered Juncker to produce 10 Guerrilla Warfare Badges in gold-plated hallmarked silver with diamond-encrusted swastikas, for presentation as personal gifts to those who had won the Oakleaves to the Knight's Cross for their achievements in counter-guerrilla operations. The only real contender for such an award would have been von dem Bach, but he did not receive the Oakleaves and, so far as is known, none of those alleged diamond-encrusted pieces has ever been seen.

All originals of the rare Guerrilla Warfare Badge which the author has seen have been identical in construction to the example illustrated, being crisply cast in zinc with an appropriate coloured wash. The reverse is semi-hollow, and does not feature a mirror-image of the obverse design. There is no maker's mark. The needle pin is of steel, with a brass barrel-hinge of typical Juncker type and brass retaining clip.

There are at least 11 fake variations of the Guerrilla Warfare Badge in circulation, some solid and others hollow, in brass, bronze, nickel silver and aluminium. It is important to remember that by the time the Guerrilla Warfare Badge was instituted in 1944, these materials had been universally replaced by zinc in the manufacture of German War Badges. Any Guerrilla Warfare Badge made from a metal other than zinc should be viewed with the greatest suspicion. Some reproductions have broad, flat pins and others bear makers' marks, including 'C.E. Juncker, Berlin', 'CEJ', '2' (the code for Juncker) and 'L56'. A 'de-luxe' version of the Gold grade, in solid brass with a blued steel sword blade and silver pin has been reported, but probably falls into the same category as the 'de-luxe Close Combat Clasp in Gold with top hook' which appeared at militaria fairs in the late 1980s and which turned out to be a fake from the same stable as the so-called Silver Clasp for Female SS Auxiliaries.

The reason why so many good reproductions of the Guerrilla Warfare Badge are about can be explained simply by the rarity of the original item and the consequent high prices commanded. The following list gives details of examples of the award recently offered for sale in the UK, with the prices sought. Where the badges concerned were actually viewed by the author, an opinion as to their originality or otherwise is also given. As can readily be seen, price does not necessarily equate with originality!

December 1987	Silver grade	£350	Fake
December 1987	Gold grade	£650	Fake
May 1990	Gold grade	£750	Original
October 1991	Silver grade	£495	Not seen
October 1992	Silver grade	£585	Not seen
December 1992	Bronze grade	£375	Fake
January 1993	Bronze grade	£420	Fake
January 1993	Bronze grade	£8	Fake
March 1993	Bronze grade	£350	Original
June 1993	Gold grade	£350	Fake
August 1993	Bronze grade	£465	Fake

5 Reproductions, Fakes & Fantasies

The biggest problem faced by collectors of Third Reich items is the proliferation of postwar copies which have flooded the market since the 1950s. The Waffen-SS field has been particularly hard hit in this respect, due to the inherent scarcity of original pieces and their correspondingly high values. However, it is equally true that British, US, Rhodesian, South African, Polish, Chinese, French, Russian, Israeli, Spanish and even mercenary militaria has also been professionally copied, and collectors are just as likely to be 'caught out' buying these items.

The term 'reproduction' is normally used to refer to a fairly accurate and good quality copy made in the same way and using the same materials as an original. Examples include everything from hand-embroidered bullion insignia to complete tailor-made tunics. A 'fake', on the other hand is something of lesser quality, which has the general appearance of an original but does not bear close inspection. Converted modern German army peaked caps and water-transferable helmet decals would fall into this category. The lowest of the low are the 'fantasy' pieces – crude modern productions which have no factual basis at all, like the 'SS-Fallschirmjäger' cuff title and enamelled metal wall plaques bearing Waffen-SS divisional insignia. Most collectors feel that postwar copies, whatever their quality, are things to be avoided and would rather possess an original example of a common item than a reproduction of a rare one. Nevertheless, even the most prestigious and well-respected museums now include some reproductions in their displays, having unwittingly purchased them at auction or had them donated over the years.

Since the early 1980s, various publications have appeared, primarily in the UK and France, showing the whole range of Waffen-SS uniforms being worn by models in life-like settings, and all in 'glorious colour'. One or two even go so far as to suggest that the staged photographs should be used to help the collector identify the genuine from the fake. However, while much of the field equipment and many of the other items used to illustrate these books are undoubtedly original, a large proportion of the uniforms and insignia are unquestionably reproductions. For example, one figure has been depicted wearing the Aircraft Destruction Badge, which was never made or issued during the Third Reich, while another very youthful SS-Untersturmführer is shown sporting a lengthy fake ribbon bar which includes the NSDAP and SS 25-year long service awards. Some of the less accurate copies used to illustrate these publications are explained away by the assertion that they must have been 'made in the East'. They probably were – but in the 1980s! On no account, therefore, should modern 'reconstruction' reference books be used as the sole means of determining the authenticity of any piece.

The old-fashioned, methodical study of large numbers of wartime photographs still provides the best indication of what Waffen-SS uniforms and insignia should look like. After going through thousands of such pictures, the author has yet to come across a single one depicting the so-called variant Dutch-made 'Adolf Hitler' cuff title, or the wide metal collar patch runes allegedly produced in occupied Poland, or the M44 tunic manufactured from Zeltbahn material, or the SS paratroop smock. Original photographs clearly demonstrate a

132

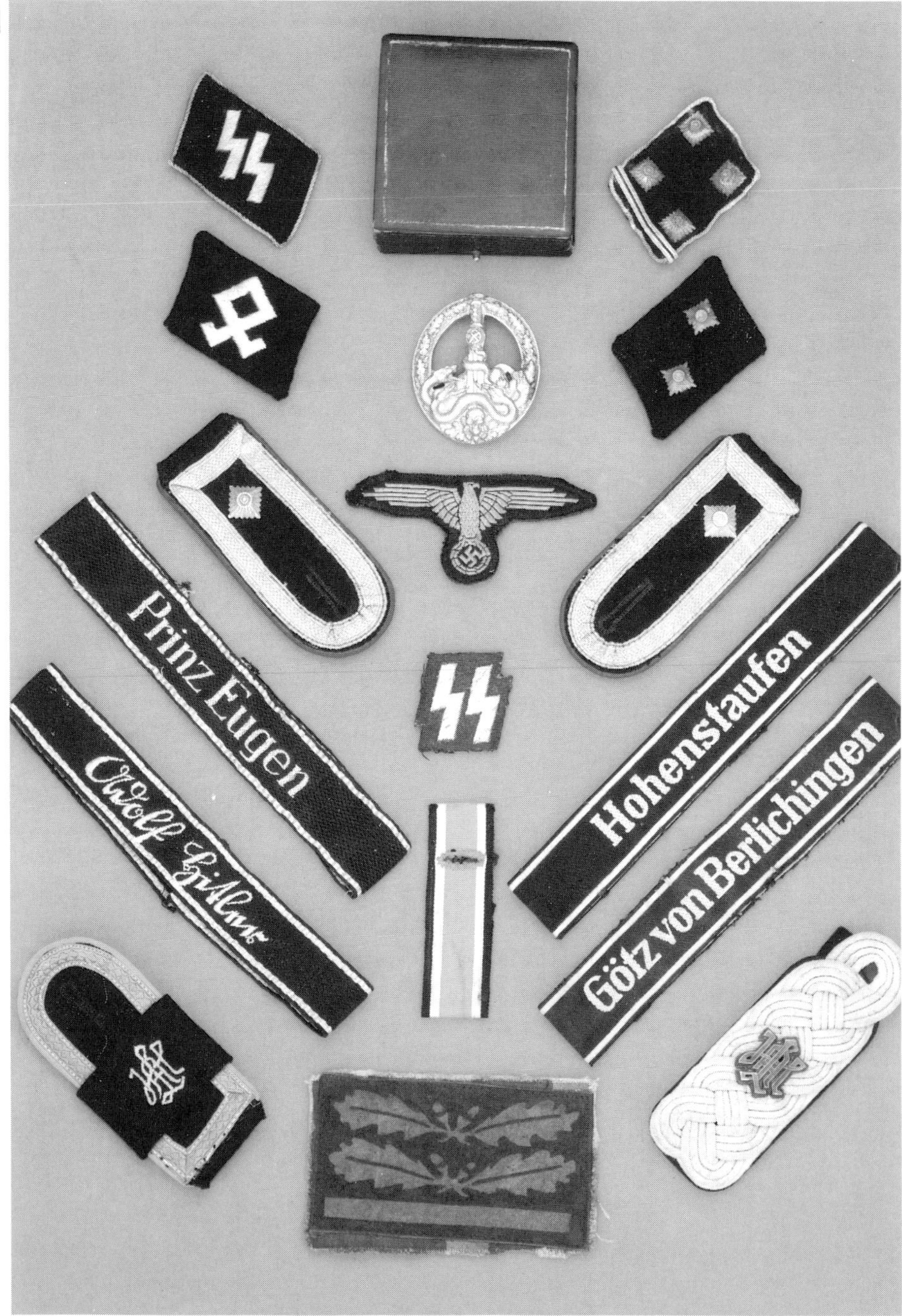

Plate 132: *An impressive display of Waffen-SS items. But are they all original?*

Plate 133: *Fake Waffen-SS General's peaked cap, with aluminium piping. The band is in dark grey wool instead of the correct black velvet. Note also the spurious hand-embroidered bullion eagle, and the Prussian death's head in soft lead-based alloy.*

133

remarkable consistency in the production of Waffen-SS uniform items. Tunics, headgear and badges remained standardised right up until the end of the war, albeit that some individuals chose to wear army eagles or other non-regulation insignia from time to time. The simple fact is that a general misconception has evolved that SS uniform was subject to extreme variations in quality and appearance during the 1944-45 period, and that misconception has helped the fake merchants to peddle their wares.

All the main categories of Waffen-SS militaria have been the subject of reproduction, and each can be considered in turn with a view to fake detection.

The quality of original Waffen-SS peaked caps was always good, but the materials used in their construction varied from one manufacturer to another. Cap crowns or bodies could be in wool, ribbed twill or moleskin, and interior linings ranged from rough waterproof hessian fabric to exquisite silk. Sweatbands were usually in soft leather, although an ersatz pressed paper substitute was also used after 1942. A thin, semi-brittle, transparent celluloid sweat shield was stitched inside every cap crown, and normally carried the maker's details.

Early fake Waffen-SS peaked caps were produced by converting their West German military or police counterparts, often simply by removing the Federal insignia and replacing it by reproduction SS badges. Externally these fakes were fairly convincing, but internally they could be readily distinguished by their having one or more of the following characteristics:

(i) Thick, soft, pliable sweat shields
(ii) Nylon linings neatly machine-stitched into place, rather than being loosely hand-stitched into position like originals
(iii) Polyurethane sweatbands with a vinyl-like appearance
(iv) Plastic foam padding in the cap body
(v) Chin cords with plastic components instead of the wartime steel, zinc or stiffened leather
(vi) Plastic chinstraps
(vii) West German issue date stampings or 'DBGM' marks

During the 1980s, a range of superb quality reproduction Nazi peaked caps was manufactured, encompassing everything from army, navy and Luftwaffe pieces to HJ and Allgemeine-SS examples. Caps in this series were custom-made from scratch, with such niceties as bogus RZM labels and hand-stitched linings. Of course, the Waffen-SS did not escape the faker's attention

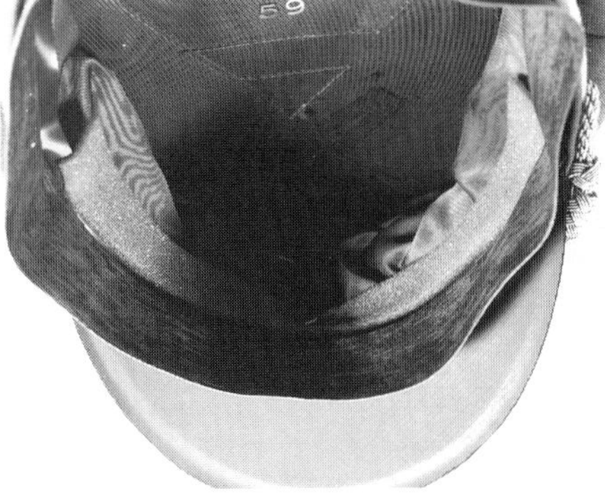

134

Plate 134: *Interior of a fake peaked cap. Note in particular the give-away plastic foam sponge padding. The sweatband is of polyurethane, vinyl-like in appearance, and the shiny nylon lining is neatly machine-stitched behind a plastic beading strip around the sweatband.*

135

Plate 135: *Fine quality reproduction Waffen-SS officer's peaked cap, made of woollen material with a velvet band and leather peak. The shiny new chin cords are slightly too small, while the zinc alloy eagle and death's head both bear the code mark 'RZM 360/42 SS' and are typical of the badges manufactured in Austria during the 1980s.*

and variants with piping in all the Waffenfarbe colours were duly completed. The general give-away with these items is their overall 'mint' condition, with no natural ageing, fading or weathering. The 'musty smell' so characteristic of originals is absent, and they feature heavily nickel-plated reproduction insignia and bright new chin cords. Some have old original interiors fitted.

To complicate matters still further, a few genuine but standard Waffen-SS peaked caps have been 'doctored' over the years to pass as scarcer versions, by using colourfast marker pens to transform their ubiquitous white SS piping into 'Panzer pink', 'concentration camp brown' and so on. If converted properly, these items can be difficult to detect since the caps themselves are patently original. However, authentic piping should always be cleaner under the sides of the cap than along the front and back, where it will have been exposed to the sun and the elements, and Waffenfarbe piping which does not show any colour tone variation may be suspect. Obviously, any piping which reveals a white base should be viewed with alarm!

Field caps, particularly the Einheitsfeldmütze, have also been widely reproduced and the latest copies are distinguishable only by virtue of their fake insignia and immaculate condition. Very few original field caps survive unused, for even those which were never issued to soldiers during the war were quickly distributed to civilians after the capitulation. Ventilation grommets in mint condition, with unchipped paint on the outside and shiny tin securing washers on the inside, are a sign to be cautious. Moreover, instead of the correct RB or SS-BW numerical ink markings, fake field caps are often stamped with elaborate makers' details in the form of 'pseudo trademarks', an example being '59 - Otto Schlientz, Uniformmützen, Straubing - 1944' around the central design of a schirmmütze. Mis-spellings, like 'Braunsweig' instead of 'Braunschweig', have even been observed in the composition of these trademarks.

The surest signs of originality so far as cloth headgear is concerned are well-worn, sweat-stained interiors and dirty, faded exteriors. In any case, most collectors desire to see some 'age' about their caps, preferring pieces that were worn on campaign to those which spent their war lying on a tailor's shelf.

The same holds true for field tunics, which have again been professionally reproduced. All wartime field blouses were made from a coarse, heavy woollen/rayon

136

Plate 136: *Excellent modern copy of an SS fez, in maroon coloured woollen material. The superb quality BEVO insignia is let down by its slightly blueish hue, and there is no regulation sweatband.*

Fig 20: *A selection of reproduction and 'fantasy' insignia offered by a British dealer in 1993. Of particular interest are the Italian SS eagle with fasces at top right, and the British Free Corps 'three lions' collar patch and Union Jack arm shield at centre left.*

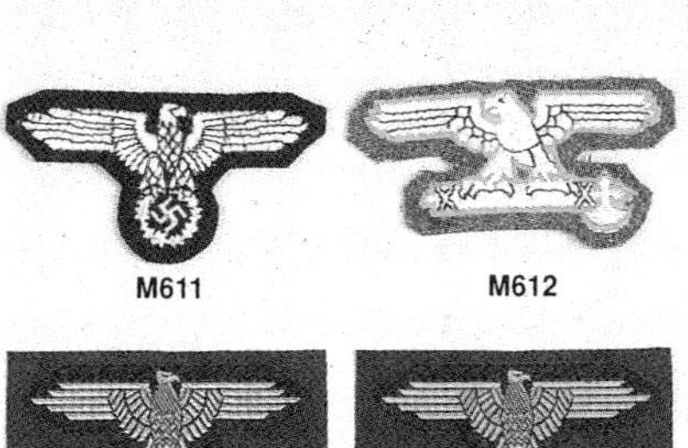

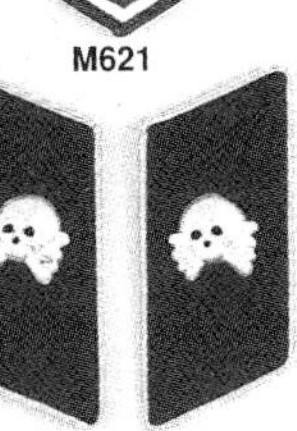

FIG 21

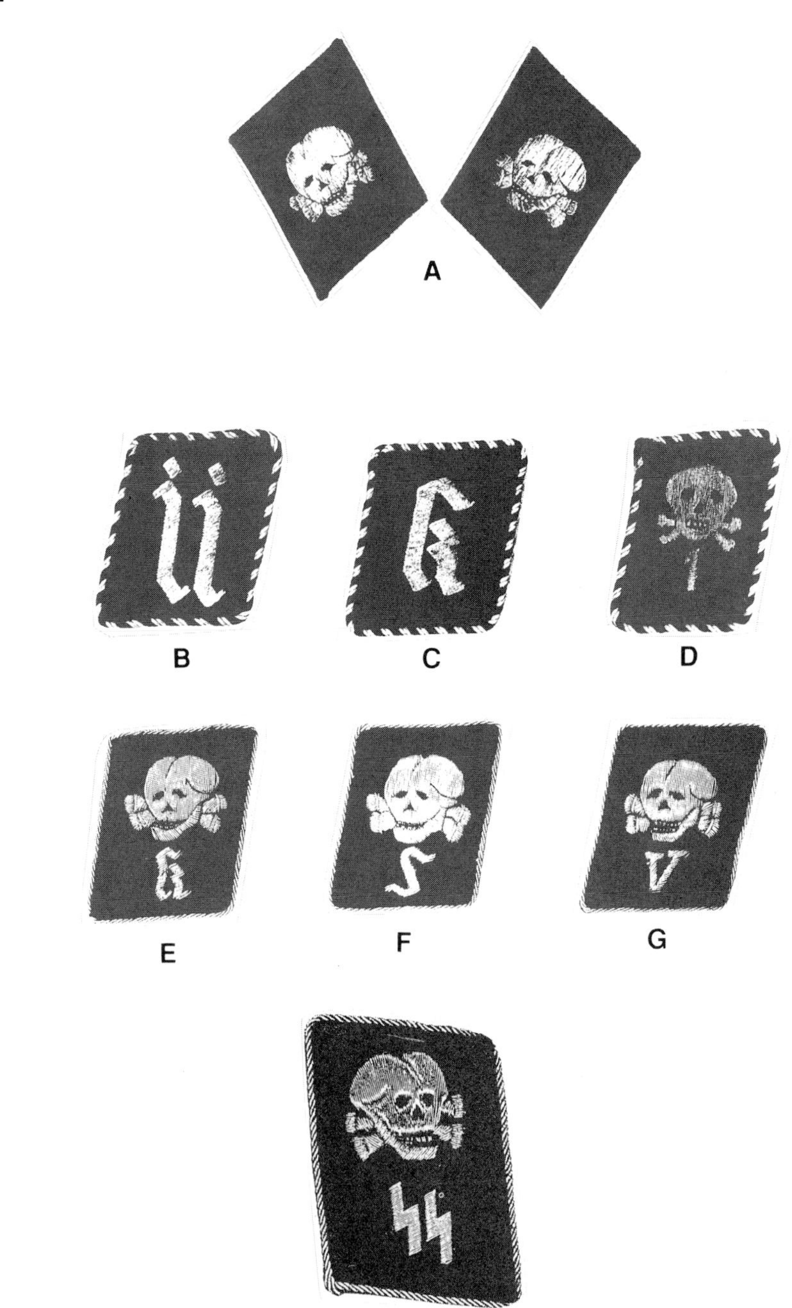

Fig 21: *A selection of reproduction death's head collar patches, showing the variety of copies available and the high standard of their manufacture. Those depicted relate to:*

A SS-Totenkopf-Division (1939-40)
B Dachau training camp (1934-37)
C Concentration camp staff (1934-37)
D 1st SS-TV company (1936-40)
E Concentration camp staff (1937-40)
F SS-TV medical battalion (1936-40)
G 5th SS-TV battalion 'Brandenburg' (1936-37)
H Fantasy piece created after 1945

cloth and were partially lined in rough cotton twill or artificial silk. Copies tend to be fully lined in nylon, and lack the distinctive 'zig-zag' pattern of stitching which invariably featured under original collars. It should be borne in mind that Waffen-SS and police combat uniforms were generally made in concentration camp factories using confiscated and reprocessed materials, and it is not uncommon to find original tunic sleeves lined in a 'candy-stripe' or other patterned cloth which may formerly have been part of a shirt or dress. Hand-stitching is also a good sign, as camp seamstresses tended to finish garments off by hand in the traditional way.

Officers' dress tunics constitute a more difficult area, as originals were made from a variety of fine materials, were fully lined, and often incorporated distinctive differences in cut to meet the wide-ranging tastes of buyers. Above all, few genuine dress tunics show any real signs of age as they were seldom worn. The best reproductions have original buttons, but since wartime insignia is not usually available to the fakers they have to make do with good quality copy badges, which duly expose the tunics for what they really are.

Fakes of every type of Waffen-SS camouflage item are also in circulation. A small number are recognisable as such because they are made in the wrong type of material, or have an inappropriate camouflage design. Examples include helmet covers, field caps and smocks in denim drill fabric rather than the correct waterproof cotton duck, and reversible winter jackets and mittens in 'pea' pattern instead of the original autumn camouflage. The majority of copies, however, are more realistic.

Smocks, in particular, have been expertly reproduced, and since early copies often used material cut from genuine Zeltbahns the sole method of fake detection lay in the manner of their construction. The body of each original smock was produced from a single strip of fabric with a central hole to accommodate the head and neck, in a poncho fashion. Consequently, the front and back comprised one continuous piece of material, with no stitching from the neck across the shoulders to the top of each arm. Moreover, wartime smock sleeves were formed from two or three strips of material, made into 'tubes' and sewn together. Early fakes were identifiable by the fact that their bodies comprised two separate pieces of fabric, one front and one back, joined together by stitching across the shoulders, and their sleeves were generally made from a single strip of cloth. The latest reproductions are manufactured and cut in the correct way, but from brand new cotton duck. They are recognisable simply by their pristine condition and bright colours.

Copies of helmet covers and camouflage field caps have also been made in realistic new fabric to original specifications. The bogus helmet covers usually lack the large bare aluminium securing rivets which were so typical of originals, while the fake field caps are lined in grey cotton complete with spurious makers' marks.

The Model 1944 drill uniform in 'pea' pattern camouflage has been liberally reproduced to order, for members of the battle re-enactment fraternity. Copies are often waterproof, unlike the real thing, and are typically very dark brown in appearance with light tan, yellow and green spots in fresh, unfaded colours. The interior of each garment is white and unlined, and is minus the regulation belt hook supports, field dressing pockets and size stampings. Some bear a faked version of the SS-Bekleidungswerke mark, comprising the letters 'SS-BW', often in a rectangle, without an accompanying code number. A few 'deluxe' copies of the drill tunic with pleated patch pockets, like those on the Model 1936 army field blouse, have also been produced in recent years, possibly modelled on a unique privately purchased version worn by Paul Hausser during the Normandy campaign. It should be noted that

137

Plate 137: *A Waffen-SS officer's tunic, the originality of which is debatable. With quality such as this CAVEAT EMPTOR applies.*

original 'pea' patterns were often badly registered during the machine-printing process, resulting in the basic fabric colour, a grey-white, showing through in a 'highlight' effect around some colour edges. Such flaws must not, therefore, be regarded as indicative of a reproduction.

The camouflage drill version of the Waffen-SS Panzer uniform has also been faked, but cut in the army style with a slanted front, large pointed collar and lapels, and a central seam down the back. Some of these copies are composed of up to three different patterns of material, are fully lined in cotton or artificial silk, and sport tan-brown tropical arm eagles.

In general terms, very little original Waffen-SS camouflage material survives, and most of it is in a worn and faded condition. Any piece showing bright colouring and no 'wear and tear' must be viewed with extreme caution, even if it was allegedly 'found in a warehouse in Russia last year'!

Fake Waffen-SS collar patches dating from the 1960s and early 1970s were usually fairly poor quality affairs, often with felt or rough woollen bases. Silver bullion hand-embroidery was crude and misshapen, machine-embroidery was excessively thin and sketchy in appearance, and rank pips were invariably cast in soft, lead-based metal or brittle, glittery alloys. One series of copies encompassed a whole range of odd collar patches, including various

Plate 138: *Runic collar patches: an original pair (top) and two fake pairs (centre and bottom). The originals bear the two rank bars of an SS-Rottenführer but are of officer-quality manufacture, being hand-embroidered in fine aluminium thread on a soft flexible imitation velvet base. It was not uncommon for enlisted ranks to wear officer type badges, which they could purchase at their own expense. The fake pair at centre also depict the rank of SS-Rottenführer, but there all similarity ends. The runes are hand-embroidered in a bright, thick silver bullion which is prone to tarnishing, are mis-shapen with rugged edges and lie at the wrong angle, while the rank bars are in a spurious twisted silver bullion wire. The base is a heavy black woollen material reinforced with cardboard so that it does not bend easily. The pair of reproduction collar patches at bottom, for the rank of SS-Schütze, are better copies in the correct black cloth. The runes are machine-embroidered like originals, but are too large, extending almost to the top and bottom edges of the patch.*

138

alleged non-Germanic types such as the Tartar wolf's head and Indian tiger's head which were said to have been found unissued in the Dachau clothing stores in 1945.

Reproductions made in the 1980s were far more realistic and today's fakers wisely concentrate on the standard German SS collar patches rather than the more 'exotic' foreign types which immediately arouse suspicion. The SS runes patch, death's head patches and senior officers' rank patches have all been copied in cotton thread or fine aluminium wire on woollen or velvet backings, and are exceptionally difficult to detect. The best reproduction Totenkopf variants are of particularly good quality and are much in demand and very saleable, even at extortionate prices. Indeed, they frequently fetch more than 100 times their cost of manufacture. Former East German army rank pips, in die-struck white aluminium with thin brass wire attachment prongs, feature on many current sets of reproduction SS collar patches, and are far more convincing than their earlier fake counterparts.

Collectors must be extremely cautious of any SS collar patches offered in mint condition, even if they are advertised as 'still stitched to an old piece of collar'. Death's head patches are really best avoided altogether, so great are the odds that they will be reproductions. Colour fading, oxidation and natural weathering are

Plate 139: *Reverse views of items shown in* **Plate 138**. *The originals (top) have the patch edges wrapped around a fine canvas core, while the fakes at centre are glued on to stiff cardboard backings. The reproductions below have glossy white paper centres over which the borders of each patch are folded.*

139

still the best indicators of originality, although it should be borne in mind that even the poor quality copies of the 1960s may now show some considerable signs of age.

Fake shoulder straps are characterised by their extensive use of thin black felt. Copies of other ranks' and NCOs' versions usually lack any form of field-grey woollen reinforcement on the reverse of the upper portion, which originals generally had, and often feature a backing of shiny grey-green artificial silk material instead. Reproductions of officers' straps commonly sport easily-obtainable white aluminium rank pips of the East German variety, rather than the correct style of gilt or bronze pips which are more difficult to come by.

The reproduction of both embroidered and woven Waffen-SS cuff titles has been especially prolific and lucrative, and in this area quality is usually fairly good. There are many varieties of fake, but most of them fall into one of the categories listed below, which should enable collectors to identify them.

(i) Roughly hand-embroidered in silver bullion: original aluminium wire hand-embroidery was always finely executed with each letter distinctly formed
(ii) Hand- or machine-embroidered on to a thick rayon band with six-strand aluminium wire borders: genuine rayon bands were relatively thin and almost always had seven-strand borders. There are exceptions to any rule, and a seven-strand border is by no means a guarantee of authenticity, but in general terms an embroidered cuff title with six-strand borders is very likely to be a postwar copy
(iii) Machine-embroidered on black ribbon: the latter was never used in the manufacture of original cuff titles
(iv) BEVO-woven in a coarse cloth: originals were woven in thin artificial silk, which was flimsy to the touch
(v) BEVO-woven with very smooth borders: the threads on BEVO originals were slightly rough, giving a 'serrated' look to the borders under magnification
(vi) BEVO-woven with a white reverse: genuine BEVO examples had a black-and-white chequered effect on the back
(vii) BEVO-woven with no loose threads behind the wording: originals always had loose threads at the back
(viii) BEVO-woven with bogus RZM tags: such labels were never encountered on wartime woven cuff titles. However, many did feature the maker's mark 'BEVO-Wuppertal', in small letters as an integral part of the weaving at each end of the band. This mark has also been reproduced on some
(ix) Crudely embroidered in chain stitching: alleged 'Dutch-made variants' of the 'Frundsberg' and 'Hitlerjugend' cuff titles with chain stitch lettering were manufactured in the 1970s

In addition to reproductions of official SS cuff titles, a number of fantasy pieces which had no authentic Third Reich counterparts are also in circulation. These include the following titles, none of which existed before the end of World War 2:

Berlin	Nibelungen
Böhmen-Mähren	Otto Skorzeny
Britisches Freikorps	Schill
Dachau	Seelager
Dirlewanger	SS-Fallschirmjäger
Galizien	SS-Kavallerie -Division
Junkerschule Tölz	SS-Polizei
Kaminski	Totenkopf I
Karstjäger	Totenkopf II
KTL der SS	Totenkopf III
Leibstandarte	Ungarn
Lettland	Wallonie
Lützow	

Waffen-SS arm eagles in all their forms have been copied extensively and in a variety of qualities. Early reproductions were in light blue thread on black felt, and easily detected. However, current fakes of the regulation machine-embroidered pattern, particularly the late war 'round-headed' type, are often fairly accurate. Some tend to feature quite thin embroidery with too much of the black background showing through between the wing and chest feathers, and on others the length of the wings is too short in proportion to the body height. A few embroidered fakes follow the design of

Plate 140: *Three fake Waffen-SS other ranks' arm eagles. The item at top is machine-embroidered in white cotton thread on a field-grey woollen base, and is a 1988-manufactured fantasy derived from the design of the SS pennant eagle. The eagle at centre is finely machine-woven in black and white artificial silk and is a very accurate copy of the BEVO SS arm eagle, let down by its deformed swastika. The item at bottom is machine-woven in a thicker synthetic silver-grey and black rayon, and is a poor representation of the BEVO eagle. Note the short fat wings, pronounced head and the crudely wreathed swastika which is too large.*

140

the BEVO eagle, with the wreath around the swastika comprising properly-formed oakleaves instead of the plain circle characteristic of all machine-embroidered originals. Most reproductions of BEVO-woven eagles are exceptionally fine, and in many cases are almost indistinguishable from the real thing. Nevertheless, the majority of BEVO copies are offered for sale in mint condition on their uncut backings, and that is always a sign to be cautious. Hand-embroidered fake bullion eagles, usually emanating from India and Pakistan, tend to have very 'heavy' wings which are too wide and leave the eagle's head 'submerged' between them.

The following fantasy SS arm eagles were created in the late 1980s:

(i) The pennant-style SS eagle, machine-embroidered in black and white cotton thread on a field-grey woollen base
(ii) The Italian-style SS eagle with fasces, machine-embroidered in black, white and red cotton thread on a field-grey woollen base
(iii) The BEVO-style SS eagle, machine-embroidered in grey cotton thread on camouflage material.

(These are readily identifiable by virtue of their own unique forms.)

141

Plate 141: *Reverse of items shown in* **Plate 140**. *The embroidered eagle at top is backed with a black hessian material. The item at centre, so convincing from the front, has on its reverse a rectangular 'block' weave pattern of a type never encountered on originals. The lower badge, on the other hand, while inaccurate in its design, has the correct weave pattern on the reverse.*

Reproductions of every type of SS headgear insignia have appeared over the years, including those detailed below:

(i) Helmet decals of the water-transferable variety, which can easily be damaged by scratching with a thumb nail

(ii) Cap eagles and death's heads poorly stamped in tombakbronze, with wide triangular prongs on the reverse

(iii) Cap eagles and death's heads in readily-bendable lead-based alloy, with flat prongs on the reverse and the spurious makers' codes 'RZM 3/8' and 'RZM 40'

(iv) Cap eagles and death's heads in readily-bendable aluminium, with round prongs on the reverse and occasionally the maker's mark 'RZM 5/8'

(v) Cap eagles and death's heads in sturdy aluminium with flat brass prongs on the reverse and the maker's code 'RZM 360/40 SS'

(vi) Cap eagles and death's heads in zinc alloy, with flat brass prongs on the reverse and the maker's code 'RZM 360/42 SS'

(vii) Cap eagles and death's heads in heavily nickel-plated alloy, with thick round prongs on the reverse and the makers' codes 'RZM 41' or 'RZM 52'

(viii) Cap eagles and death's heads in silver, stamped '800'

(ix) Cap eagles and death's heads in grey plastic

(x) Death's head buttons for the M34 Schiffchen, with two rows of teeth to the skull (original buttons had only one row)

(xi) Cap eagles hand-embroidered in silver bullion on field-grey or black woollen cloth

(xii) Death's heads in grey BEVO-weave, with the skull's right eye socket in a vertical rather than horizontal position and the 'BEVO-Wuppertal' mark

(xiii) Cap eagles in grey BEVO-weave, with rounded heads and a 'zig-zag' pattern to the chest area

(xiv) Cap eagles and death's heads BEVO-woven in green and tan-brown

(xv) The one-piece cap eagle/death's head insignia crudely machine-embroidered on a field-grey, black or spurious camouflage background

(xvi) The one-piece cap eagle/death's head insignia BEVO-woven in grey thread on a field-grey or black background, with only one row of teeth to the skull (originals had two rows)

(xvii) Cap eagles and death's heads hand-embroidered in gold bullion

While the fakers always tended to concentrate on the lucrative areas of collar patches, shoulder straps, cuff titles, arm eagles and headgear insignia, various other SS badges have also been copied. These include sports vest insignia, unit cyphers, the whole range of foreign volunteer arm shields, mountain troop edelweisses, Old Campaigner's chevrons, the runes worn below the left breast pocket and the rank insignia for camouflage clothing. Copy piping and tresse for collars and shoulder straps is available by the metre, and even BEVO-woven RZM labels have been reproduced for sewing on to bogus uniforms and badges.

Moreover, dozens of other miscellaneous Waffen-SS collectables have been faked. Belt buckles in aluminium or silver-plated brass, with a variety of spurious makers' marks including SS runes in a diamond and the code 'OLT/62637' (which was actually the faker's initials and telephone number!), have been around for some time, as have reproduction cap cords, tunic buttons, sword knots and so-called 'SS-Heimwehr Danzig I.D. discs'. A more recent fantasy piece is the 'Waffen-SS Police Flag', comprising a yellow police eagle on a green and white quartered field, all printed on synthetic material with brass eyelets. The production of imaginary SS rings has also proven profitable, with items like the 'Wiking Division Ring', which features a viking's head and runic shields, selling widely. The only officially authorised and truly authentic SS ring, the SS Death's Head Ring or Totenkopfring, has been reproduced to such an extent that virtually every one now offered for sale is a copy. The prices of these fakes range from £5 to £500, and one enterprising dealer in Germany even made rings to order in the 1980s! Collectors who are offered examples of the Totenkopfring should beware the following points, which characterise the copies:

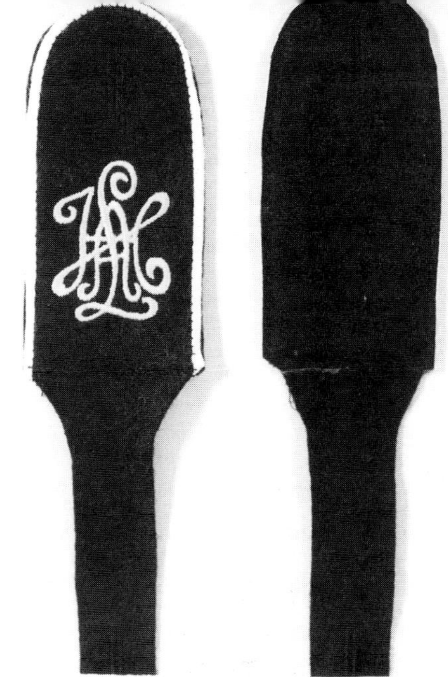

142

Plate 142: *Reproduction shoulder straps made entirely from felt, with the prewar monogram of the Leibstandarte.*

(i) An '800' or '935' silver hallmark – these did not appear on originals
(ii) Himmler signatures which are stamped instead of engraved
(iii) The SS motto 'Meine Ehre heisst Treue' engraved inside the band instead of the proper inscription
(iv) Sig-runes at the back of the ring
(v) A blank cartouche at the back of the ring
(vi) Nickel or zinc rings instead of the correct solid silver
(vii) Casting or pock marks
(viii) Inscriptions in Gothic lettering
(ix) The teeth of the skull not properly defined
(x) RZM or SS proof marks inside the band of the ring – never a feature of originals

Waffen-SS recruiting posters, Wehrpasses, Soldbuchs, driving licences, postcards, photographs and even song books have been reprinted. To authenticate bogus citations and paperwork, a series of fake and fantasy rubber stamps evolved, and these now include the following titles:

'Schutz Staffeln – Quartier, Berlin sw/68'
'SS-Polizei'
'SS-Totenkopf Division'
'Vrijwilliger Legioen Nederland – 2 – Den Haag'
'Waffen-SS'
'Waffen-SS – Kommundantur der Amts. Kztn.-Lager Cublin'
'Waffen-SS – Verwaltung – SS-Flak-Ers.-Abt.'

The majority of these stamps are absolutely meaningless, and spelling mistakes like 'Kommundantur' instead of 'Kommandantur' and 'Cublin' instead of 'Lublin' demonstrate the faker's lack of knowledge. Some stamps even erroneously incorporate the word 'Briefstempel', which should only appear on a document and never on a stamp itself! Death's heads, runes, the SS motto, belt buckle designs, RZM/SS labels and Himmler's signature have all been produced in the form of perspex and rubber stamps.

Convincing new fakes regularly appear from time to time, with plausible 'pedigrees' designed to assist their acceptance. In 1992 for example, a 'batch of SS uniform thread' was allegedly 'found in the former East Germany' and rolls of it, complete with RZM labels attached, circulated widely on the collectors' market. Suspicions were soon aroused, however, by the sheer quantities of thread available, and these suspicions were duly justified when one buyer cut his newly-acquired roll of thread open to reveal the words 'Made in Bombay' stamped inside. Yet another 'Eastern Bloc find' had been exposed!

It would be a near impossible task to describe all the different types of reproduction, fake and fantasy Waffen-SS material which have been manufactured since 1945, but the foregoing should give the reader a good idea of the extent of the problem and the main points to look out for. The uniforms, badges and equipment issued to the German army, navy and Luftwaffe during the 1939-45 period were usually made in exactly the same way as those worn by the Waffen-SS, so an examination of the more common items of Wehrmacht militaria can provide an excellent basis on which to determine the originality or otherwise of rarer SS pieces. The best general advice is to avoid anything of poor quality or in mint condition, read up on the subject, and stick with that good old 'gut feeling'. In the end analysis, genuine differences of opinion as to authenticity will inevitably arise on occasion, and it is the buyer alone who must be satisfied in his own mind that what he is getting is the real thing.

The values of original items are always increasing and the list below shows a selection of catalogue prices which were asked by a variety of dealers for allegedly genuine pieces of Waffen-SS militaria during 1993. Despite the large sums of money involved, a number of the items offered were very dubious indeed, which only serves to highlight the fact that collectors interested in this field must be extremely careful to avoid being well and truly 'ripped off'.

Item advertised	*Price in £ Sterling*
Doubledecal M42 steel helmet	1,560
Single decal M42 steel helmet	975
NCO's M38 'crusher' field cap with cloth peak	1,105
Officers 'crusher' field cap with leather peak	1,300
Concentration camp officer's peaked cap	1,820
Artillery officer's peaked cap	1,540
Panzer officer's peaked cap	1,105
Cavalry officer's peaked cap	1,105
Feldgendarmerie NCO's peaked cap	815
NCO's peaked cap	1,075
Other rank's M34 Schiffchen field cap	490
Other rank's M40 Schiffchen field cap	425
Panzer other rank's M40 Schiffchen field cap	425
Camouflage field cap	230
Other rank's M43 Einheitsfeldmütze	385
Panzer other rank's M43 Einheitsfeldmütze	585
'Handschar' Division fez in maroon	490
'Handschar' Division fez in field-grey	390
SS-Totenkopf-Division tunic, rank of Untersturmführer	1,690
SS-Totenkopf-Division tunic, rank of Rottenführer	1,105
M43 field tunic, rank of Unterscharführer	880
M43 field tunic, rank of Oberschütze, with 'Hohenstaufen' cuff title attached	1,205
Grey-white cotton drill fatigue tunic and trousers, with 'Reichsführer-SS' Division stampings, rank of Unterscharführer	650
Panzer other rank's tunic and trousers	3,445
Reed-green denim panzer tunic, rank of Obersturmführer	1,300
Greatcoat, rank of Obergruppenführer	975
Camouflage zeltbahn	390
Early pattern camouflage smock	890
Late pattern camouflage smock	1,625
Camouflage steel helmet cover	325
Camouflage reversible winter jacket	1,280
Camouflage reversible winter trousers	845
Camouflage mittens	230
'Pea' pattern camouflage panzer tunic and trousers	1,820
Full set of insignia for an Oberscharführer of the 'Prinz Eugen' Division	2,600
Pair of Obergruppenführer collar patches	520
Pair of Untersturmführer collar patches	247
Single Obersturmführer rank collar patch	45
Single 'SS/B' collar patch in aluminium wire	285
Single death's head collar patch in aluminium wire	325
Single other rank's SS runes collar patch	100
Single other rank's 'Handschar' Division collar patch	100
Single other rank's Italian fasces collar patch	125
Pair of shoulder straps for Sturmbannführer of mountain troops	210
Pair of shoulder straps for Obersturmführer of panzer troops	130
Pair of shoulder straps for Concentration Camp other ranks	175
Single shoulder strap for Unterscharführer of transport troops	60
Single tropical shoulder strap, rank of Unterscharführer	50
Single SS-VT shoulder strap for other ranks	45
'Adolf Hitler' cuff title	425
'Das Reich' cuff title	390
'Der Führer' cuff title	490

Item advertised	*Price in £ Sterling*
'Florian Geyer' cuff title (shortened)	110
'Germania' cuff title	425
'General Seyffardt' cuff title	455
'Hitlerjugend' cuff title	715
'Osttürkischer Waffen-Verband der SS' cuff title	325
'Reichsführer-SS' cuff title	475
'SS-Schule Braunschweig' cuff title	555
'Totenkopf' cuff title	520
'Wiking' cuff title	545
Other rank's embroidered arm eagle	85
Other rank's BEVO arm eagle	60
Other rank's BEVO arm eagle for tropical tunic	50
Officer's BEVO arm eagle	130
Officer's embroidered arm eagle in aluminium wire	195
BEVO eagle for vehicle pennant	100
Metal eagle, for peaked cap	60
Italian SS metal eagle with fasces, for peaked cap	70
Metal death's head, for peaked cap	100
BEVO eagle, for other rank's field cap	100
BEVO death's head, for other rank's field cap	65
BEVO death's head, for other rank's tropical field cap	65
BEVO death's head, for officer's field cap	130
One-piece triangular eagle and death's head insignia, for other rank's M43 Einheitsfeldmütze	60
Edelweiss for other rank's Bergmütze	85
Rottenführer arm chevrons	35
Rottenführer arm chevrons for tropical tunic	20
Officer's breast runes	175
Edelweiss for other rank's tunic	85
Italian fasces arm shield	125
Croatian arm shield	125
Estonian arm shield	125
'Skanderbeg' Division arm shield	65
Flak Helper's printed arm triangle with SS runes	60
Signals trade patch	60
Sleeve insignia for camouflage clothing, rank of Gruppenführer	195
Sleeve insignia for camouflage clothing, rank of Unterscharführer	60
SS 4-year service medal	165
SS 8-year service medal, in case	455
SS 12-year service swastika, with ribbon	910
SS 25-year service swastika, without ribbon	1,235
Reichsführer's Sword of Honour, named to an officer of SS-Standarte 'Deutschland'	3,705
Other rank's belt buckle	100
Other rank's belt and buckle	195
Officer's belt buckle	295
Officer's leather belt and buckle	975
Officer's brocade belt, without buckle	325
Other rank's ID disc	40
Album containing 100 photographs relating to the SS-Standarte 'Deutschland'	845
Wehrpass to member of the 'Frundsberg' Division	195
Soldbuch to member of an SS-Polizei Regiment	100
Citation for Iron Cross 2nd Class, named to an SS-Sturmmann in a Totenkopf unit	195
Single decal M42 steel helmet	975
Citation for the SS-Totenkopfring, named to an Untersturmführer in the 'Das Reich' Division	325
Recruiting poster for the 'Wallonien' Division	165
RZM/SS paper label	25
Waffen-SS money token	85
Ceramic dish marked 'Waffen SS'	100
Plated dinner fork stamped 'SS-Reich'	35

WHERE TO OBTAIN WAFFEN-SS MILITARIA

The following militaria dealers generally carry some Waffen-SS items in stock and offer money-back guarantees. However, a few also trade in reproductions — so CAVEAT EMPTOR!

Alan Beadle
Antique Arms
PO Box 1658
Dorchester
Dorset DT2 9YD
(Tel: 01308 897904)

Blunderbuss Antiques
29 Thayer Street
London W1M 5LJ
(Tel: 020 7486 2444)

Central Antique Arms
7 Smith Street
Warwick CV34 4JA
(Tel: 01926 400554)

Adrian Forman
PO Box 163
Braunton
Devon EX33 2YF
(Tel: 01271 816177)

M. & T. Militaria
The Banks
Bank Lane
Victoria Road
Carlisle
Cumbria CA1 2UA
(Tel: 01228 31988)

Military Antiques
11 The Mall
Antiques Arcade
359 Upper Street
Islington
London N1 0PD
(Tel: 020 7359 2224)

Military Endeavours
18 Longcroft Park
Beverley
North Humberside HU17 7DY
(Tel: 01428 869086)

Nicholas Morigi
14 Seacraft Road
Broadstairs
Kent
CT10 1TL
(Tel: 01843 602243)

The Old Brigade
10(a) Harborough Road
Kingsthorpe
Northampton NN2 7AZ
(Tel: 01604 719389)

The Treasure Bunker
21 King Street
Glasgow
G1 5QZ
(Tel: 0141 552 4651)

Ulric of England
6 The Glade
Stoneleigh
Epsom
Surrey KY17 2HB
(Tel: 020 8393 1434)

The dealers listed issue catalogues featuring a range of books on the Waffen-SS:

The History Bookshop
77-81 Bell Street
London NW1 6TA
(Tel: 020 7723 2095)

Imperial Publications
PO Box 5
Lancaster LA1 1BVQ
(Tel: 01524 66660)

Landmark Books
21 The Garstons
Great Bookham
Surrey
KT23 3DT
(Tel: 01372 450780)

Motor Books
33 St Martins Court
London WC2N 4AL
(Tel: 020 7836 5376)

BIBLIOGRAPHY

Angolia, J. R.; *Cloth Insignia of the SS.* (Bender, San Jose, 1983).
Lavish illustrative history of the development of SS badges

Barker, A. J.; *Waffen-SS at War.* (Ian Allan, Shepperton, 1982).
Good coverage of Waffen-SS battles during World War 2

Bender, R. J. and Taylor, H. P.; *Uniforms, Organisation and History of the Waffen-SS, Vols 1-5.* (Bender, San Jose, 1969-83)
A good reference on unit histories and insignia, for the first 20 Waffen-SS divisions

Borsarello, J. and Lassus, D.; *Camouflaged Uniforms of the Waffen-SS, Vols 1 & 2.* (ISO, London, 1986-88).
Photographic study of SS camouflage

Buss, P.H. and Mollo, A.; *Hitler's Germanic Legions.* (McDonald & Jane's, London, 1978)
An illustrated history of the western European legions of the Waffen-SS, 1941-43

Davis, B.L.; *Waffen-SS.* (Blandford, Poole, 1985)
A basic photographic history

Gilbert, A.; *Waffen-SS* (Bison, London, 1989).
An excellent illustrated history

Harms, N. and Volstad, R.; *Waffen-SS in Action.* (Squadron/Signal, Texas, 1973).
A general pictorial account

Holzmann, W.K.; *Manual of the Waffen-SS.* (Bellona, Watford, 1976).
Basic reference on Waffen-SS uniforms and equipment

Hunt, R.; *Death's Head.* (Hunt, Madison, 1979).
A combat record of the SS-Totenkopf-Division in France, 1940

Kumm, O.; *Vorwärts Prinz Eugen!* (Munin-Verlag, Osnabrück, 1978).
An illustrated history of the SS division 'Prinz Eugen'. German text

Littlejohn, D.; *Foreign Legions of the Third Reich, Vols 1-4.* (Bender, San Jose, 1979-87).
Includes sections on the non-German units of the Waffen-SS

Lucas, J. and Cooper, M.; *Hitler's Elite.* (McDonald & Jane's, London, 1975).
The story of the Leibstandarte-SS 'Adolf Hitler'

Lumsden, R.; *Third Reich Militaria.* (Ian Allan, Shepperton, 1987).
A collector's guide

Lumsden, R.; *Detecting the Fakes.* (Ian Allan, Shepperton, 1989).
How to spot reproduction Nazi regalia

Lumsden R.; *The Black Corps.* (Ian Allan, Shepperton, 1992)
A collector's guide to the history of the SS

Lumsden, R.; *The Allgemeine-SS.* (Osprey Men-at-Arms, London, 1993).
A general history of the uniforms of the SS

143

Plate 143: *A set of reproduction BEVO-woven cap eagle and death's head insignia, dating from the late 1980s. The eagle is identifiable by its rounded head and 'zig-zag' pattern to the chest area. The totenkopf is also very distinctive, with the right eye socket in a vertical rather than horizontal position.*

Mollo, A.; *A Pictorial History of the SS, 1923-45.* (McDonald & Jane's, London, 1976).
Excellent photographic record of the SS

Mollo, A.; *Uniforms of the SS, Vols 1-7.* (Historical Research Unit, London, 1969-76).
The best series of books available on the subject of SS uniforms

Pallud, J. P.; *Ardennes 1944: Peiper and Skorzeny.* (Osprey, London, 1987).
The Waffen-SS involvement in the Battle of the Bulge

Pia, J.; *SS Regalia.* (Ballantine, New York, 1974).
Includes good colour illustrations of Waffen-SS collectables

Quarrie, B.; *Hitler's Samurai.* (PSL, Cambridge, 1983).
A history of the Waffen-SS

Quarrie, B.; *Hitler's Teutonic Knights.* (PSL, Cambridge, 1978).
A history of the Waffen-SS panzer divisions

144

Quarrie, B.; *Waffen-SS in Russia.* (PSL, Cambridge, 1978).
A photographic account of the SS on the Eastern Front

Quarrie, B.; *Waffen-SS Soldier, 1940-45.* (Osprey, London, 1993).
A history of the tactics and actions of the SS infantryman

Simpson, K.; *Waffen-SS.* (Bison, London, 1990).
Photographic history of the Waffen-SS

Smith, J.H. and Saris, W.; Headgear of Hitler's Germany, Vol 2. (Bender, San Jose, 1992).
Covers Waffen-SS headdress

Stephen, A. and Amodio, P.; *Waffen-SS Uniforms in Colour Photographs.* (Windrow & Greene, London, 1990).
Imaginative reconstructions of Waffen-SS uniforms in wear

Wilson, K.; *SS Headgear: A Collector's Guide.* (Reddick, Texas, 1990).
Many colour pictures of Waffen-SS headdress

Windrow, M.; *The Waffen-SS.* (Osprey, London, 1982).
A general history of Waffen-SS units and campaigns

Plate 144: *The reverse characteristics of a genuine Waffen-SS other ranks' belt buckle (above) and a reproduction (below). The steel original is die-struck and unmarked. The aluminium fake bears spurious RZM and diamond-shaped SS proofmarks, accompanied by the code 'OLT/62637'. It also has a 'C'-shaped catch soldered into position, which was never used on original aluminium buckles.*